10 GIFTS
—OF—
Heart

10 GIFTS
— OF —
Heart

What Your Child
Needs to Take to Heart
Before Leaving Home

SALLY CLARKSON

Whole Heart Press
Monument, CO

10 Gifts of Heart

© 2013, 2017 by Sally Clarkson

Published by Whole Heart Press
A division of Whole Heart Ministries, Inc.
PO Box 3445, Monument, CO 80132
www.WholeHeart.org

Adapted from *10 Gifts of Wisdom*
by Home for Good Press

Interior design by Clay Clarkson, Monument, CO
Cover design by Pixel Studio, Bosnia and Herzegovina

Printed in the United States of America

ISBN: 978-1-888692-13-6

*Thanks to my dear and wonderful children,
my best friends, who helped me learn what it
means to have godly character as a mother.
My stewardship of your lives has taught me
more about these gifts of heart than I have
learned any other way.*

*Special thanks to Sarah Clarkson for her
brilliant, insightful ideas and help in bringing
this book to completion. I could not have done
it without you.*

*And thanks to Clay who always keeps us
organized and together.*

Love all of you lots!

You will seek Me and find Me when you
search for Me with all your **heart.**

— JEREMIAH 29:13 —

Contents

For where your treasure is,
there your **heart** will be also.

— MATTHEW 6:21 —

— INTRODUCTION —

GIFTS OF HEART

Writing the Story on Their Hearts

You are our letter, written in our hearts, known and read by all men; being manifested that you are a letter of Christ, cared for by us, written not with ink but with the Spirit of the living God, not on tablets of stone but on tablets of human hearts.

2 CORINTHIANS 3:2-3

Therefore, we are ambassadors for Christ, as though God were making an appeal through us ...

2 CORINTHIANS 5:20

We are what we repeatedly do. Excellence, then, is not an act but a habit.

ARISTOTLE

9

"**H**ow did you raise all of your children to be so self-composed and polite?" I hear that question often and it is inevitably followed by, "It must just be a Clarkson trait. It seems like it must have been just natural and easy for you." How far from the truth!

A trained heart comes only through training, instruction, and practice. Every parent wants their child to grow up into a vibrant, gracious, competent adult, yet few today have a vision for the discipline of cultivating a heart for those traits in their children. Moralistic rules and policing their behavior will not captivate their imaginations for a life with God. To raise them with true godly character, you need to capture their hearts. They need to see what you see; they need a vision for their lives.

I realized this as I worked to nurture my children early on. When Clay and I seeded their hearts with a vision for becoming confident leaders in their generation—when we trained them to become skillful at work, taught them how to be gracious and mannerly, challenged them to serve and initiate—they responded. By combining a compelling vision of what they could be with day-to-day training and encouragement, we were preparing them to become influential adults in their lifetimes, confident and gracious with the messages of Christ.

Excellence of character captivated my attention many years ago when, as a young missionary, I was challenged to move into Communist Eastern Europe to draw people to Christ. I accepted the challenge, and part of the preparation was a great deal of training. One of the pictures of ministry presented to us in our training as missionaries has stayed with me all these years and influenced my parenting—the idea that I am to be an ambassador for Christ (2 Corinthians 5:20). An ambassador is a diplomat of the highest rank chosen to represent his or her country in a foreign land. As such, ambassadors must represent the messages, values, and wishes of the country they represent. They must also maintain the highest character so their position of influence will impact the people they serve in the most positive manner for the country they represent. Paul's description of us as "ambassadors for Christ" to the nonbelieving world beautifully captures the idea: "as though God were making an appeal through us; we beg you on behalf of Christ, be reconciled to God."

I caught a picture in my young life that as an ambassador for Jesus and His kingdom, I was to represent His love by being generously loving and kind. As He is righteous, I was to be righteous—I was to practice godly integrity in front of the people I was seeking to reach. As an ambassador of Christ, I was to represent Him in every situation. Consequently, when God blessed me with children, I already had in mind that I would prepare them to become the best representatives, the best ambassadors for Christ, wherever He would lead them.

Manners, loyal love, a trained mind, a sense of God's purpose, spiritual vitality, character, gratitude—all these themes and more are present in this book. The chapters that follow are a general summary of what Clay and I considered basic training for our children for becoming effective ambassadors for Christ. Each chapter in this book covers some aspect of how we encouraged our children to godliness, equipped them with the tools they would need to be strong in spiritual battle, and enabled them to live and love well as followers of Christ and as His ambassadors to the world.

This book is about some of the ways we set about to deliberately instill in our children an understanding of their identity in Christ that would prepare them for life, whether for times of blessing and bounty or times of doubt and challenge. It's about how we formed them, and their faith, with the biblical character and skills they would need to flourish, even in a fallen world, as mature adults and vibrant souls. It's about how we gave them a heart for God—for His kingdom and His righteousness.

Many children today learn principles of morality, yet they enter adulthood without the kind of intentional training that will help them be faithful in a hard life. I am sharing with you a picture of my vision for parenting that shaped and strengthened my children's faith—the kinds of training, habits, truths, and rhythms that would prepare them to stand strong, both in the storms of a darkening world, and for the beauty of a life with God. It is what we did to give our children a heart for God that would prepare them to be "lights in the world, holding fast the word of life" (Philippians 2:15-16).

Strength does not just happen naturally, and certainly not easily. In the same way that an athlete must exercise his muscles to develop physical strength, so we must exercise our spiritual muscles to develop strength of character. It is not a perfect science and it does not happen all at once any more than working out one time lasts you for a lifetime. Personality differences, abilities, gifts, experience, and a host of other factors, means that we will be stronger in some areas than others, and vice versa. Yet, the practice of training the heart will indeed produce a lifetime of fruit in your children, and in your life as a parent as well.

Everything we do in our children's lives in the brief time they are with us is, as Paul said, like writing a letter on their hearts, "not with ink but with the Spirit of the living God," that will be "known and read by all men" (2 Corinthians 3:2-3). What your children become once they leave your home will, in many ways, be your living letter to the world of what is most important in your own heart. Like Paul, we should remind and affirm our children as they prepare to leave our homes: "You are our letter" and "we are ambassadors for Christ." That is, after all, the heart of godly parenting.

This book is not meant to be a comprehensive plan or theology for giving your children a heart for God. That doesn't exist. It is, though, a picture of the kind of family life and parenting that will enable you to influence your children, shape their lives, build their character, and form their faith. And that is where they will learn what a heart for God looks like and they will follow your model. It's an organic model—if you create the right kind of soil, good things will grow there.

Consider this book a kind of compact training guide for future ambassadors for Christ. It's not everything that needs to be said, but it's enough. It will prepare you, as a parent, to prepare your children, as future ambassadors, to live for Christ. To have the kind of heart for God that will enable them to stay faithful once they leave your home.

I hope you will find in reading this book a potluck feast of stories, thoughts, suggestions, and encouragement. But mostly, I hope you will find principles, practices, and truths that will enable you to prepare your children to have confidence, a sense of calling, and a heart for God to walk the roads He brings their way.

May all of our children be worthy ambassadors for Christ and His kingdom.

Sally Clarkson
May, 2017

Selecting the Gift

What is the Story I will write on my child's heart?

Trust in the LORD with all your **heart**
and do not lean on your own understanding.
In all your ways acknowledge Him,
and He will make your paths straight.

— PROVERBS 3:5 —

CHAPTER 1

A HEART FOR FAITH

The Gift of Living Spiritually

Therefore as you have received Christ Jesus the Lord, so walk in Him, having been firmly rooted and now being built up in Him and established in your faith, just as you were instructed, and overflowing with gratitude.

COLOSSIANS 2:6-7

Mother is the name for God in the lips and hearts of little children.

WILLIAM MAKEPEACE THACKERAY

Ask any of my children about their enduring memories of childhood and one of them is bound to mention family devotions. They still chuckle about the Alpha and Omega day when I drew an overview of Scripture on a chalkboard and told my ten-, eight-, and six-year-old children that God was the beginning and end of all things and their lives were part of his story. "Will you live by faith?" I passionately asked, and was met by their wide-eyed nods.

To this day, twenty-four years later, they still remember that epic morning devotional. But more than just that one morning, they remember the rhythm of faith and prayer that shaped all our days as a family—there were no days when God was not with us.

They also recall the way that faith became real when they saw God actually answer our prayers. One particular morning stands out in all of our memories. The early years of Whole Heart Ministries required us to trust God for something new almost every day. We moved to the middle of nowhere, Texas, lived with my mother-in-law, and began to outline and write the messages we wanted to give to parents.

Our lives were all by faith then—believing, praying, and trusting that God would direct our nascent ministry and provide for our needs. He certainly seemed to be blessing our ministry, for which we were very thankful, but there came a time when the ministry (and, therefore, our family) was one month away from running out of funds. I remember one morning at that time very clearly.

It was a sunny Texas day, and my children were laughing and fussing, squirming in their breakfast chairs. We didn't tell the kids everything, of course, but we wanted them to be part of this life of faith, trusting God whether in plenty or in need. When we came to prayer at the end of our devotions, we told them simply that we needed to see God provide financially for our family. Would they pray that too?

Their little faces grew very solemn (although this did not in the least stop their squirming). They squeezed their eyes shut and held their hands tightly together where they sat at the table and each of them prayed in their high voices that God would give us what we needed.

Clay went straight to his office after breakfast, and the kids and I finished the dishes and gathered in the living room to start our day. But before we could begin, Clay was back with news of an amazing discovery. On picking up the morning mail, he found in a national news magazine the story of a particular class action lawsuit settlement regarding a failed investment he had written off long before we were married.

Because we'd been overseas and moved multiple times, Clay never received a notice about the lawsuit. But the article said that there was still one week left to file a claim before the lawsuit was closed. He did, and the amount we received would adequately meet our need for funds for months to come. When we told the kids, their eyes were wide with wonder at the fact that God had answered their prayers.

"Mom," said Sarah, "God really heard us, and it worked. Isn't that amazing?"

❤

The most important gift you can give your child is to help them begin a walk of faith with the God of the universe. From the moment your children arrive in your home, you are teaching them how to see the world—what to consider important, what to believe, what to seek, what to love. As a mother, you have the opportunity to form your home and family life in such a way that God's reality comes alive to your children each day.

We live in a busy, pragmatic society driven by performance and activity. As mothers, we particularly feel the pressure to provide the best of everything for our children—training, education, lessons, activities, friends, even meals. We want our kids to have character, clean their rooms, excel in school, have the best music lessons, be in all the activities they want, and to never be lonely.

You can fill up your child's life with good people, good activities, and good things, but that will not be enough. What your child needs most is a heart that knows the love of God. The greatest gift you will give your children, a gift they will carry with them into every relationship and situation of their lives, is a heart deeply centered on loving God and loving others, and a mind formed and filled by the habits of faith.

For me, as a mom, it was all about a kingdom mindset—an awareness of my life, and my family, as part of the ongoing story of God's kingdom breaking into this world all around us, and how we could be part of it. That's why Jesus taught us not to worry about tomorrow, which will always take care of itself, but rather to "Seek first His [God's] kingdom and His righteousness" (Matthew 6:33-34).

Your first priority as a mother is to introduce your children not just to truths about God, but to His reality in their lives. You are helping them understand what it means to seek His kingdom and His righteousness every day—to love Him, to know Him, to believe in His presence, to see His work in the world around them, and to form their lives according to His truth and will. They won't learn all that in Sunday school or Bible club. It is in your home and in your presence that your children will learn what it means to be a follower of Christ and a seeker of God and His kingdom. They will believe what they see in you.

The kingdom life is a spiritual life—a life lived in the power of the Holy Spirit. It is lived out as a rule of life—the practice of a way of seeing life by the Spirit ("the mind set on the Spirit is life and peace," Romans 8:7), and a habit of prayer that sets God and His kingdom at the center of all you teach and do. Paul affirmed that "in Him [God] we live and move and exist" (Acts 17:28). The life you create in your home can communicate this reality every day. But it is vital to remember that this kind of spiritual life isn't just a list of rules you and your children must keep. It is living life in the Spirit of the living God.

The kingdom life at home is a life centered on a relationship with God, an awareness of His presence, and love in the smallest details of your family. Though it is not about rules, it includes cultivating habits of faith—making time each day for family and personal devotions, praying together regularly, reading and memorizing the Scriptures, encouraging one another in the faith.

But it is more than just good habits. It is also a way of life—a celebration of who God is, what He is doing, and how we fit in. This life includes watching for His beauty in the changing of the seasons, thanking Him for life or health or unexpected grace, feasting on holy days, and cultivating a constant awareness of God's goodness at work in the world. It is the "life and peace" from the Spirit of God that Paul envisions.

That is a beautiful vision of family life. However, you as a mom cannot give what you do not have. Before you can pass this kind of life for God on to your children, you need to know that kind of life yourself. Just like you need to know Scripture before you can teach it to your children, you need to know God before you can show Him to them.

Whatever it takes, you must plan for ways to nourish your own spirit, to keep your own heart close to God, to find the life in the Spirit that Scripture promises to believers. For me, that meant getting up before my kids for a cup of coffee and some quiet time with God. It meant planning specific hours when I could get away to read about others who follow God, or simply to unburden and rest my spirit. It meant finding spiritual fellowship with like-hearted friends.

Regardless what else you do, you must do whatever it takes to set aside a space of time each day to pray, to read Scripture, to journal—to seek God. You also need encouragement and accountability, so seek out friends and mentors who will keep you accountable in your walk with God. If like-minded souls are hard to find, start a Bible study or fellowship yourself. Read. Pray. Seek. The goal is to be sure that your own heart is rich so that when you teach your children you can give to them out of your own treasure.

One of the sweetest gifts of my life is to watch my grown children walk with God. I have asked them why, despite the foibles or failures of our family, despite struggle and imperfect days (and imperfect parents), they caught the faith we were trying so hard to teach them. I find in their answers that it was the spiritual rhythms of our lives, the relational connections between us all, the atmosphere of love and grace, and the way of making God present every day in our home that shaped them most.

"I loved God because of crisp bacon and French toast and real maple syrup," said Sarah one day. "We ate and celebrated and enjoyed the goodness of God's world. And as we did we talked about God, we prayed for what we needed, we admitted our struggles, we watched Him work. Faith wasn't just a subject on the side; it was our whole life."

The gift of a whole life of faith was exactly what I hoped to give my children. I don't think there's a greater one that I could give.

❤

GIVING THE GIFT OF FAITH

In the whole life of faith, one of the best ways to begin is simply to establish a rhythm of family habits that keep your home centered on God. The whole idea of these habits is that they are a regular heartbeat in the life of your home. The following habits are practices that will help provide a framework of spiritual cultivation to your days as a family.

Family Devotions

From the time the kids were little, Clay and I made sure that every day, for a family devotion time, we read Scripture (however simple) and prayed with them. These times never looked quite the same from one month to the next, but they always accomplished the same thing. When we were all at home, Clay might read through a family devotional with lots of interaction (that was his devotional sweet spot). Other times, if he was not able to be there because of work. I would read through *The Child's Story Bible* by Catherine Vos, or read from my own Bible, and we always ended in prayer (that was my sweet spot). Either way, our goal was to begin each day with Scripture and prayer—to listen for and learn about God, and to pray to Him with praise, confession, thanks, and requests. Here are some ways that might help you accomplish the same thing in your home:

> **Make a time:** Set aside a time each day—at a meal, before bedtime, early in the morning—when you can meet for devotions as a family without distractions. Be

sensitive to how long and how much is right for your children at their ages. The more consistent you are with the time, the more time your children will learn to give to the devotions.

Plan ahead: Have a devotional or personal reflection ready to share with your kids. There are a variety of children's story Bibles available that make a wonderful and winsome way to expose your children to the stories of Scripture. We loved *The Child's Story Bible* by Catherine Vos. If they had been around in our family's childhood days, we also would've enjoyed *The Jesus Storybook Bible* by Sally Lloyd-Jones, and *The Action Bible* especially for our boys.

Be flexible: Don't worry about perfection. Most times Clay and I did devotions together, but sometimes we would trade off on leading. Each family will look different, so do what is right for you and your family. There is no doctrine of devotionals in Scripture, so enjoy your freedom, and your children will enjoy the variety. Make your rhythms and your love of God unique to your own family's time and needs.

Family Prayer

Clay and I made prayer a habit in our family from the beginning because we wanted our kids to see us believing in God, seeking His guidance and help, and acknowledging the reality of His Spirit and kingdom in our lives. We taught our children to go to God about anything—personal wants and needs, matters about friends, family concerns, missionaries, special requests, praise, thanks. Prayer was one of the main ways we regularly exposed our children to the reality of God, letting them voice their own hearts to Him, and then watching Him work in their lives. And yes, your children will squirm and have a hard time keeping their eyes shut. Mine still do as adults! But fear not—the practice and the grace of those prayer times is deeply forming your children's hearts.

Make a time: Set aside specific times each week to gather and pray as a family. Let each child share their own needs or concerns first without any parental commentary. Only then, as parents, share your own needs and the needs of your family. Expect everyone to pray, and to enter by faith together into talking to God about needs and desires. All requests are equally important.

Keep a prayer list: Make a prayer list and display it where it can be visible to everyone (not just on your digital device!)—paper on the fridge, whiteboard or chalk board on the wall, a journal on the table. Date each entry, note who it is by, and give a brief description of the prayer or request. This is a great way to remember to pray for missionaries, sponsored children, or friends with special needs. Make a special time each week to read through and pray for those on the list, and to note answered prayers to thank God for.

Pray at bedtime: Even my adult kids like to be prayed for before they go to bed. This can be a dear, comforting, and very memorable time for children in which you help them to remember God's love and comfort as they go to sleep. The habit of bedtime prayer can become an anchor for faith.

Pray always: Praying on the spot, especially in a crisis situation, is a discipline that needs to be learned. Whatever the situation that needs prayer, if you will remember to "just pray" it will be a powerful ministry in your child's life. When one of your children is struggling with doubt, or a friendship has been lost, or money is needed—just pray! You will be teaching your children that they can turn to God in every situation, and to take their needs and hurts to Him.

A Personal Bible

When your child is old enough to read and appreciate it, give him or her a Bible of their own. It doesn't need to be a big, leather-covered, serious Bible that can be intimidating and mysterious. There are lots of good, full-text Bibles available now that are child-friendly and appealing, so help them choose one that they will value and enjoy. The serious Bible can wait until they are older.

Suggest readings: Encourage your new Bible owner to make time each day to read it (even if it's mostly pictures). Give them a list of your suggested readings they can put in their Bible—Psalms, the Gospel of John, Bible stories, key passages. You'll help them create a habit that will undergird their faith for the rest of their lives.

Story Bible starter: If a full-text Bible is too over-whelming to a child, start them on one of the many story Bibles available now. This is not a step down, but a step towards—it is training to prepare them for a "real" Bible.

Family Day Celebration

Every August, on a Saturday near our wedding anniversary, we and all our children celebrate what we call our "Family Day." We start the day with a family day favorite—my homemade whole wheat cinnamon rolls and cold milk for dunking. The Family Day celebration starts with a reading of Joshua chapter four, where the Israelites are instructed to create a memorial of twelve stones so that, "When your children ask their fathers in time to come, saying, 'What are these stones?'" they will remember God's faithfulness, power, and sovereignty for them (Joshua 4:19-24). Then, as a family, we begin to share all the ways that God has been faithful to us in the previous year—jobs found, friends made, prayers answered, money provided, gifts received, dangers averted, health healed, blessings acknowledged. These are all written down on a sheet, and when everyone has shared all they want to share, we begin to assign the "memorial stones" to family members. We actually used river rocks our first year, but we quickly learned they're too hard to write on and awkward to store. So, each person ever since then gets several sheets of special paper on which to draw their pictures of God's faithfulness, and those become the memorial stones. Through the years, we have collected the lists and drawings into an overstuffed binder. It is a marvelous history of our family and a record of God's faithfulness to us for over thirty years.

"Parent and Child" Times

The best way for children to learn how to love God is through the friendship and discipleship of their parents. In addition to family devotions, Clay and I made specific personal times each week to meet individually with our children. We listened to their doubts and fears, rejoiced in their joys and victories, sought to draw out what was going on in their growing hearts and minds, read hero tales together, or talked about what it meant to be a godly young man or woman. These were informal times together—low on structure but high in influence.

Make the time: Create a time each week or two to meet one-on-one with each child. Get it on your calendar. Make it a casual and informal time of delight. If your daughter loves tea, make tea and scones just for the two of you. Sons might enjoy a pizza and soda night out with dad. Or take a more active child to play with them in the park. A special place makes a special memory to be sure, but the time is more important than the place. If you can't go out, you can still make the time special by spending it with your child.

Read together: Find a book or story that you can read aloud together that communicates some of the spiritual principles you want to teach. You could read a history or Bible hero tale aloud, a classic children's fiction story, or a story from Scripture. You could work through a special devotional book or study together and discuss the ideas each week. The time together will enhance whatever you choose to read.

Talk time: Sometimes, you just need to make time for your child to talk—to feel the freedom and safety to say whatever is in their heart and mind. This can often be a spontaneous and unplanned time that is not a part of your schedule. Always be prepared to adjust your schedule and respond to your child—you might not have a second chance to hear what your child needs to talk about. Use these times to let your child know how special they are to you, and how much, regardless of what they are sharing, you and God care for them and accept them just as they are.

Be Patient

"Train up a child in the way he should go, even when he is old he will not depart from it" (Proverbs 22:6). "Old" here suggests entering adulthood. The spiritual training you give your children to help them follow God and become mature adults forms them little by little, year by year. Don't despair if it takes time. Keep the larger vision in view.

❤

Wrapping Up the Gift

I will give my child a heart for Faith by:

_____

_____

_____

_____

_____

_____

_____

_____

_____

_____

_____

_____

_____

_____

_____

_____

Perfume and incense bring joy to the **heart,**
and the pleasantness of one's friend
springs from his earnest counsel.

— Proverbs 27:9 NIV —

CHAPTER 2

A HEART FOR FRIENDSHIP

The Gift of Faithful Fellowship

Iron sharpens iron, so one man sharpens another.

PROVERBS 27:17

Friendship is the greatest of worldly goods. Certainly to me it is the chief happiness of life. If I had to give a piece of advice to a young man about a place to live, I think I should say, 'Sacrifice almost everything to live where you can be near your friends.' I know I am very fortunate in that respect.

C. S. LEWIS

As the sun set, casting shadows around our kitchen as I made dinner, my little girl walked in slowly and sat at the kitchen counter. Tears welled up in her round, brown eyes as she put her elbows on the counter and held her face in her hands.

"Mama," she started, and it all came tumbling out. "I thought that Christians were supposed to be different. I can't believe my friend would lie to me and then get mad at me for talking to her about it. It just doesn't seem fair!"

The whole story eventually came out through stops and starts of tears and sniffles. The cause of Joy's woe was a very close friend who had gotten angry, yelled harsh words, and stomped out when Joy tried to talk to her about a sensitive issue. I came around the counter and held my heartbroken daughter closely, helping her to wipe her eyes.

"How about we have a cup of tea together and talk about it?" I asked.

With candles lit a few minutes later, hot chocolate chip cookies ready to be dunked in milk, and tea steeping, I sat down with my sweet girl as she settled in on the couch.

"Mama," she started, "you've always quoted that Proverb about 'a friend loves at all times.' I didn't really know what that meant until tonight. Gossip and fighting and drama are awful. I don't really feel like loving, but that verse means I'm supposed to be committed to my friend, no matter what, right? Just like Jesus is committed to us, even when we sin against Him."

I nodded and squeezed her hand as her tears flowed again. She smiled a wobbly smile and leaned close to me.

"It really costs a lot to be a good friend, doesn't it, Mom?"

❤

Friendship is an extraordinary and often costly gift from God, a beautiful reminder that we are not expected to do life alone. When we teach our children the value of true friendship and fellowship, encourage them in creating community, and help them to know how hard it will be, we are giving them the gift of learning to love well. We are instilling the skill of faithful, forgiving, and cultivating love that will equip them to flourish on the unique journey that God has for them.

Through the many joys, struggles, successes, and major disappointments that life may bring, it is a great gift to have community around us, to have godly friends. But it is a gift that must be chosen, nourished, and sometimes renewed. Dietrich Bonhoeffer described the concept of Christian community eloquently in his book *Life Together*. He says this:

"Christian community is like the Christian's sanctification. It is a gift of God which we cannot claim. Only God knows the real state of our fellowship, of our sanctification. What may appear weak and trifling to us may be great and glorious to God. Just as the Christian should not be constantly feeling his spiritual pulse, so, too, the Christian community has not been given to us by God for us to be constantly taking its temperature. The more thankfully we daily receive what is given to us, the more surely and steadily will fellowship increase and grow from day to day as God pleases."

As mothers, we have the powerful opportunity to teach our children the great value and worth of friendships. The way we model, encourage, and create fellowship is crucial to the way our children will learn to relate in their own adult lives. I never wanted my children to see themselves as loners, as people not responsible to love and bless others. I wanted them to perceive themselves as givers, as hosts, as true friends.

We were made to know God's love through the love we give and receive. We were made for close family friendships, for community, for relationships that last throughout our lives. But friendship is something we must fight to create. The hectic nature of modern life, the increasing isolation caused by technology, and just the inherent risk of dealing with sinful human nature causes many people to draw back into isolation.

If you can teach your children to reach out, to be the ones who make connections, who truly see other people and voice their love and care, you will have equipped your children both to receive and give love in a powerful way. They will be able and equipped to offer love to a world that desperately needs it.

But raising children who will value friendship in this world is no easy task. Friendship has to do with the major heart issues we have to face in ourselves and in our children—knowing how to love, to forgive, to be kind, to be patient, to nourish relationships, to put others first. The hardest part comes as we teach our children to put others first. Thinking of ourselves and doing what we feel best satisfies us is natural; putting others before us, being humble, thankful, and selfless, is supernatural. As Jesus reminds us, "Greater love has no one than this, that one lay down his life for his friends" (John 15:13).

I had my children memorize that verse. I knew that ideas like that, memorized and remembered, could call out truth to my children throughout the day. Mothers may sometimes feel overwhelmed and exhausted with these minuscule, routine, daily words of truth that we must speak over the lives of our children.

However, my ministry began as a mother by simply taking the time and having the patience to offer one word, one prayer, and one instruction at a time to the little ones who so desperately needed my direction. That's how hearts are formed, minute-by-minute and word-by-word.

You are the first example of friendship your children encounter. They need this friendship as a foundation and model for other friendships that will come in their lives. Creating time of nurturing fellowship with my kids was just as important as training their manners or confronting their behavior. Before my children could be good friends, they needed me, their mom (and dad), to befriend them and be a friend to them.

They needed me to help them learn how to navigate the often choppy waters of friendship, to learn how to be faithful initiators. More than just being a friend, I wanted them to know how to make a friend. I invited them into special times with me, and then helped them to invite and plan special times with their friends. I taught them how to prepare for their friends—to make cookies, light candles, plan activities—so their friends would feel welcomed and loved.

In my relationship with my children I taught them forgiveness, forbearance, and a self-controlled tongue. When they came home frustrated and angry at the offense of a friend, I walked them through the process of accepting and forgiving that person. Much of my authority came from the history of the friendship I had with my child, a history filled with the very forgiveness and acceptance I was asking them to show.

Throughout their childhood, I also kept in mind that the way they saw and heard me relating to my friends would shape their own views of friendship. When we as moms view our relationships with others as a rare and beautiful gem, a gift to be treasured, we will be able to model what it looks like to nurture those friendships with a grateful heart. We will be teaching our children to honor and value others, to rise above selfishness, and to cultivate kindred spirit fellowship.

After all those years of teaching my children to invite people over, to have patience, to write thank you notes, to speak with grace, to be loving even when they didn't feel like it, I am now able to watch each of them flourish in their personal and professional friendships. They've learned how to appreciate and enjoy others, plan for times of fellowship, and reach out and engage others. It is all a gift that will go with them wherever they find themselves in life.

❤

Giving the Gift of Friendship

Teach Your Children to Put Others First

> "True humility is not thinking less of yourself; it is thinking of yourself less."
>
> ~ C. S. Lewis

As a mother, you're faced with the challenge of a world that generally teaches people to think mostly of themselves. But Jesus taught us to "love your neighbor as yourself" (Matthew 22:37), and Paul taught us to be like Christ and "not merely look out for your own interests, but also for the interests of others" (Philippians 2:2). Your task is to help your children develop a Christ-like heart, mind, and soul in a self-serving culture in which they will live as adults. Our children will adopt a "putting others first" heart only if we first help them have God's mind about selflessness. Instructing our children in what it truly means to put the needs of others first will enable them to be great friends and have great friends. How does this happen?

Set a good example: Little eyes will always be watching? You're their first model. Are you displaying an example of serving joyfully? Or do you dread putting others first and see it as a daunting task? In your own friendships, model the same behavior that you would hope your children will exhibit. As your little ones watch your interactions, they will learn and be inspired by your own selflessness.

Model opened eyes: It's so easy to create virtual "blinders" that prevent us from seeing the needs of people around us—all we see is what is right in front of us. Teach your children to open their eyes to the needs of others. Talk to them about various situations that others are in, whether friends or strangers, and about how they would want to be treated if they were in another person's shoes. Focus on the Golden Rule: "In everything, therefore, treat people the same way you want them to treat you, for this is the Law and the Prophets" (Matthew 7:12).

Model opened ears: Being a good listener is a crucial aspect of becoming a great friend. Encourage your children to follow James's advice to always be "quick to hear, slow to speak and slow to anger" (1:19). Home is a wonderful and comfortable place to practice and learn listening skills. For instance, learning how to ask questions and listen is a great way to make friends. Role-play a mock conversation with a friend by having your child ask you questions and listen to your response, and then have them tell back to you what they heard, not just in your words but also in your expressions, tone of voice, and body language. Model at home showing genuine interest in others by interviewing mom or dad about their life story, or asking siblings about their day. Make the dinner table a place and time of discovery, with each person finding out new things about the others. When we ask questions and listen, we are showing others that we care about what they have to say.

Trust the Holy Spirit

Unfortunately, a "good behavior" pill has not yet been invented. But as much as we all would find such a miraculous pill useful at times, God's solution is better—living by the power of the Holy Spirit. "[W]alk by the Spirit, and you will not carry out the desire of the flesh" (Galatians 5:16). That promise goes for your children, too. Raising selfless children in a selfish world will be an never-ending spiritual challenge. Our children will be better on some days than on others (they're still children!), just as some days are better for us as parents. Be gentle and patient with them (fruit of the Spirit in Galatians 5:22-23), and show them grace when they struggle with the very natural and human desires to be selfish or self-centered. Model for them what it looks and sounds like to trust God and to ask the Holy Spirit for help on those kinds of days. Love your children with your whole heart, even on the difficult days.

Teach Your Children to Share

"Mine" is one of the most common early words to be uttered from a toddler's mouth. From a very early age, our sweet little ones learn that something can belong to them, and shortly after comes the desire to become very possessive and controlling about almost everything in sight. Selfishness in toddlers, and the desire to make everything they want "mine," is an early attempt to set apart and create their own unique identity within the family order. This is a natural, normal process, but when bad attitudes, screaming, and tantrums come into the mix, it's also a behavior that needs training in the right direction so a child learns to become a giver, not a taker. seeing the needs of others and wanting to help. Also, it is about learning that enjoying something with a friend is better than keeping it all alone. When it comes to sharing, practice may not always make perfect, but it makes habits, that make character, that make sharing a more natural and normative part of your child's life. As children start playing with others and seeing the need to cooperate, they will learn the value of sharing. Here are some ways to cultivate a heart of sharing:

Encourage sharing with siblings: Encourage sharing by purchasing books and toys that do not exclusively belong to just one child. Of course, there are special things that each child will hold as their own. But if a general attitude of community ownership is nurtured, children will learn to hold toys, books, and possessions with open hands instead of grasping ones, and sharing will be more natural.

Encourage caring acts: Encourage your children to give toys, notes, hugs, or something of their choosing as gifts to their siblings. Help them to take what is theirs and share it with another. Consider having a once a year "clean out the toy box day" when children can choose which of their toys they want to share with someone else, or even better to donate to the less fortunate.

Teach respect of others: When your children reach an age that they are going to a friend's house to play, take some time to talk with them about what to expect and how they should behave. Talk about being respectful of others' belongings, and remind them that they are a guest in their friend's home. They should always share, but it isn't something their friend is required to do. Remind your children to be good friends, good sports, and good at sharing even if their friends are not doing the same.

Create Community

One of the first things that friendship requires is for someone to initiate. "Hey, do you want to come over for tea?" Those words can be the first in a long story of a deep and lifelong friendship. But that will happen only if you train your children to be those who initiate, who invite, who prepare for the people they love, and create a space where fellowship can happen.

Saturday pizza nights: Invite another family over once a week for an evening of talk, good food, and games. Let your children prepare in choosing a fun dessert, setting out cups and plates, lighting candles, and creating a welcoming environment for your friends. Engage them in thinking about how to make the night a good time of fellowship.

Small group meeting: Start a regular small group time with other moms who have kids close to your children's' ages to do different projects and crafts. Start an "Inklings Fellowship" like my Joy did, and discuss the works of C. S. Lewis and Tolkien. Or, start a Bible study for teen girls, or a character and camping club for boys. Foster community by bringing it into your home and let your kids help with every aspect of planning and leading the group

Friend meets: Your daughter has probably watched you have friends over for tea since she was little. Or your son has noticed his dad meeting a friend for study. Encourage your child to come up with a special time to meet with a friend, and offer to help them think about what to do with that time.

Thank You Notes

Raising my children to be people who write thank-you notes has made a significant difference in the course of their lives and friendships. Writing thank-you notes can be what sets your child apart from the rest of the crowd after an interview for college, a job, and more. But it is also a way of connecting with the people you love, affirming why you are grateful for them, and connecting with them to keep a relationship vibrant and alive. Thank-you notes also teach the language of relationship, and how to express thoughts and feelings articulately. While a digitally-connected generation may view handwritten notes as "old-fashioned," it is a special way to show respect, honor, and love to others. The more your children practice writing thank-you notes, the more confident they will become. This can be a fun, creative task and a wonderful learning experience. Take the time out of your day to sit down with your children and practice writing thank-you notes as a family. Here are some tips to get you going:

When to send: When is the right time to write a thank-you note? Anytime! There is really never an occasion, favor, or gift received for which writing a thank-you note would not be appropriate. Thank-you notes should be written:

- After someone has given you a gift of any kind
- After a special dinner, event, or occasion
- When someone has done a special favor for you
- When you want a friend to know what you think

At what age: Your child is never too young to participate in the thank-you note process. From the time my children were just learning to write (and could just barely write their own names), I would talk to them about what they were thankful for or what gift was extra special to them. Next, I would write the thank-you notes for their birthday gifts and other occasions and simply have them write their names at the bottom. They would be in charge of decorating the note, drawing pictures, and making the note "pretty." This is a wonderful way for your children to start early on the route to gratefulness.

What to include: What should I include in my thank-you note? There are no specific rules for what goes in a thank-you note, but there are some things that will increase its value to the recipient:

- Clean, neat handwriting communicates that you care about the person and what you are saying, and that you are not rushed and careless.

45

- A warm, personal greeting, with correct spelling of the name of the person you are writing, is a *sine qua non* of a proper thank-you note. It is the gateway to the rest of your note.

- As basic as it may sound, you should always express what you are thankful for in the note. If it was a gift, write specifically what the gift was and why it is so special to you. Consider including a photo of you using your gift. If it was a gift card, describe or show them in a photo what the gift card purchased.

- Affirm what you love about the gift, but also what you love about the giver. Express what they mean to you, and why you think they are special (pleas know that affirmation is not the same as flattery; everyone needs to be noticed and affirmed). A thank-you note should be just as much about the giver as it is about the gift.

- When you come to the end of your thank-you note, always include a personal closing before your signature—a personal note, a "warm regards" generic line (with love, best wishes, yours truly, and such), or a custom close that you like to use. Never close your note with only your signature.

❤

Wrapping Up the Gift

I will give my child a heart for Friendship by:

_____

_____

_____

_____

_____

_____

_____

_____

_____

_____

_____

_____

_____

_____

_____

_____

_____

Watch over your **heart** will all diligence,
for from it flow the springs of life.

— PROVERBS 4:23 —

CHAPTER 3

A HEART FOR CHARACTER

The Gift of Loving Virtue

*But the fruit of the Spirit is love, joy, peace, patience,
kindness, goodness, faithfulness, gentleness, self-
control; against such things there is no law.*

GALATIANS 5:22-23

*I hope I shall possess firmness and virtue enough to
maintain what I consider the most enviable of all titles,
the character of an honest man.*

GEORGE WASHINGTON

"**Y**ou never let me get away with a single thing, Mom!" My sixteen-year-old daughter looked at me with a dramatically tragic face and tears in her big, blue eyes. "Why can't you just understand that I'm a teenager? All of my friends have attitudes, too, and their moms let it slide. I'm just feeling emotional." Her eyes were flashing with perturbation now.

I sighed. Confrontation, especially with my children, is surely my least favorite thing in the world. All I had asked was that Sarah empty the dishwasher and load the dishes. The roll of her eyes, the mutterings under her breath ("It's always me; the boys never help") and the thump of her reluctant feet had prompted me to suggest that perhaps work was simply part of life and that she had a choice to make about her attitude.

Our confrontation at the sink, as with other mother-daughter confrontations, continued far beyond that dishwashing moment. We talked afterward. I share some relevant scriptures. I reminded her of our standards as a family. I hugged her. I encouraged her. I sent her upstairs to recover and to have some time to think and pray. And then I sat back on the couch, exhausted, knowing very well that ten such conversations might happen again the next day with four of my sweet and sinful children in the house.

❤

Moments like that were charged with some of the most important work I did as a mom. I knew then, and even better now, that I was training my children's hearts forming their faith, and strengthening their character through those confrontation.

When my babies were born, I had grand visions for them. They might be missionaries to Africa, or great writers (like Dickens or C. S. Lewis), doctors who cured cancer, or musicians (Bach? Beethoven?) who changed the world. But as I was confronted with four little ones with self-centered hearts, strong wills, and God-given gifts and natures, I quickly realized that one of the hardest but best roles I would ever play as a mom would be as a trainer of godly character.

"He who is faithful in a very little thing is faithful also in much" (Luke 16:10).

I think that biblical truth, spoken by Jesus, is burned into the brains of my children. It was one of my mantras as they were growing up. Now that they are adults, they smile as they recount how often I repeated that phrase to them. But I repeated it because I was convinced that if my children learned how to be faithful in the smallest details of life—housework, sibling relationships, parental honor—God would trust them more and more with the great deeds that needed to be done in His kingdom. And since I had decided from the beginning that I was raising kingdom-hearted heroes, I just kept on training.

As I did, and as I turned to Scripture for encouragement, I quickly realized that what I was doing as a mom was just what Jesus did with his disciples. Day after day he taught, modeled, and trained them what it meant to love and honor God. He was there to answer every question, to confront every wrong attitude, to shape every conversation. He lived every day with twelve men who would eventually change the world.

One of my glories as a mother was realizing that I had the opportunity to form the hearts and life habits of my children. Together, Clay and I had a never-to-be-repeated time to shape the faith of our children, and to train them in godliness, from their earliest years.

One of the ways we did this was to create a list of character standards for our home, family, and personal lives. Each of what we would call "our twenty-four family ways" was backed with Scripture and a character quality definition. These would become the language of biblical family values we wanted to instill in our children.

Clay was mostly responsible for the 24 ways and later turned them into a devotional and discipleship resource for families. *Our 24 Family Ways* included four easily memorized statements of biblical family values in each of six common areas of family life—Authorities, Relationships, Possessions, Work, Attitudes, and Choices. Here are a few to give you an idea of what a "way" is:

- We love one another, treating others with kindness, gentleness, and respect.

- We serve one another, humbly thinking of the needs of other first.

- We are thankful to God for what we have, whether it is a little or a lot.

- We choose to be peacemakers, even when we feel like arguing.

However, it is more than just language to learn. There are also five days of family devotional outlines for each of the twenty-four ways that we would go through together as a family—120 family devotions. Along with learning the ways, we helped our children memorize the Bible verse or passage for each way. We discussed the ways, and used them as part of our discipline and training in the home, not only for confronting sinful attitudes, but much more for encouraging good ones.

By creating a family culture based on biblical values and virtues, we created a home atmosphere for our children in which character training was simply part of everyday life, a normal expectation for our family. But that also meant that it was an every day, and almost every hour, responsibility for me as a mom. And that was hard. There were no days off from character training! If pursued with determination, it is certainly one of the more challenging tasks of being a godly mother.

With the help of God's Spirit, instilling good character in a child is the result of countless conversations enjoined, habits instilled, confrontations engaged, and daily interactions encouraged. To avoid or neglect any of those divine moments was to miss what God might have planned to accomplish.

My desire was to make the training and discipleship of my children part of the regular rhythms of my life. I wanted it to be like a constant melody I was singing throughout every day with my children—helping them take part in housework, settling fusses together, modeling and expecting gracious speech, insisting on the completion of personal tasks and responsibilities, encouraging faithfulness to finish a book or project.

The family ways were like a familiar chorus in the training song I was trying to sing in my life at home with my children. They were the notes we always returned to. I wasn't making things up on the spur of the moment, or asking arbitrary things of my kids. We all knew the values by which we wanted to live; the song we wanted to sing. We were learning to sing it together.

Another challenge I had to deal with as a mother was simply the cultural climate in which I was raising my children. Modern culture has lost the heart and art of character formation—the inculcation of classic virtues such as humility, diligence, prudence, patience, honor, and others. I miss that call to virtuous living.

We live in a world where so many things that once were considered holy are now dismissed, or even profaned. Almost anything that we as believers consider to be "good" is now a target for a growingly post-Christian culture—ungodly humor turns anything holy into a joke, sarcasm is an insidious disease of language, sexuality is as common and ubiquitous as advertising, and coarse language is accepted and infectious. Self-centeredness is the new religion of the masses, and nobility and virtue are treated as relics to be disparaged and discarded.

As I observed the increasing disintegration of Christian culture when my children were young, I knew I needed an antidote to keep that cultural disease from infecting my children's spirits. I needed to challenge the cultural narrative with one that reflected God's values. So, in order to create vivid pictures in their minds of what biblical virtue looks like in real life, I turned to the stories of historical and biblical heroes. I carefully researched to find the best-written and best-illustrated books that would engage my children's active imaginations and bring to life the kinds of heroes we wanted them to value, remember, and emulate.

We filled our home library with a wide variety of quality books by good authors about great men and women of history and the Bible. The kids pored over the "Childhood of Famous Americans" series, the "Landmark" history series, and many beautifully illustrated books about heroes of the faith and history. They also loved listening to "Your Story Hour" audio-dramas about the lives of virtuous men and women like Booker T. Washington, Abraham Lincoln, Eleanor Roosevelt, and many others. In an absence of virtuous role models in modern culture and media, we were serious about creating mental role models that would shape our children's hearts and minds for virtue, nobility, and honor.

In addition to biblical and historical books, we also read (and read aloud, and listened to on audiobooks) virtuous and beautiful children's literature such *Just David*, *Anne of Green Gables*, *The Secret Garden*, and many other similar classics. Everyone in the family also loved imaginative works of fiction and fantasy for children such as "The Chronicles of Narnia" and *The Hobbit*.

Through all these stories, we were engaging in the formation of a vibrant imagination in each of our children, an inner idea of what it looks like to be virtuous, and an inner vision to see God alive in their lives. A Christian imagination enables a child to see with the "eyes of the heart" in order to believe. We considered all these books and resources to be tools of faith formation.

❤

It delights me now when I hear my children repeat a familiar "family way" by memory, or when one of them seriously exhorts the rest of us (with a smile) that "he who is faithful in a very little thing is faithful also in much." It is so rewarding to see their character, faithfulness, and grace and honor for others now. But there is a greater delight much bigger than all those rewarding reminders of my motherly training and discipleship.

As I write this many years since that season of childhood, I know I've successfully launched four wholehearted and faithful children into adulthood who love God with their heart, soul, mind, and strength—they are strong in Christian character and godliness, committed to biblical virtues and values, seeking to serve Christ and His church, and leaning into the kingdom of God and His righteousness with their entire lives. The road to getting here, as with any family, was full of potholes and speed bumps, but we are all on the same road to the same destination. That is my greatest delight.

Are my children perfect? Of course not. And neither am I. Spend a day or two with all of us in our house and all our imperfections will become perfectly clear. But therein is the rub. Despite my own weaknesses and limitations as a mother, despite my failures and fallings, despite my own sins and imperfections, I was still able to raise my children to be godly, honorable, and virtuous men and women.

Paul exhorts parents to "bring [your children] up in the discipline and instruction of the Lord" (Ephesians 6:4). Implicit in his words is the promise that even sinful parents can raise up godly children to follow Christ. That is what makes all the training and discipleship worth the time and effort. "I have no greater joy than this, to hear of my children walking in the truth" (3 John 4).

"You never let me get away with a thing." Sarah, now an adult, said that again to me the other day. But this time, her eyes were wide and sparkling with life, and her face was gentle with gratitude. "All those times when you could've saved yourself so much stress by just ignoring my attitudes, you confronted me. You trained me. Mom, you've saved me years of misery!"

I smiled. I was just so glad she finally understood. She knew the blessing of a heart that follows God.

❤

GIVING THE GIFT OF CHARACTER

Teach Your Family Your Ways

Use the 24 Ways: Clay wrote *Our 24 Family Ways* when our children were young, but they still live in our minds and hearts as adults. We memorized them together, and used the ways and the scriptures to train our children to live in a way that would be "of the Lord" in all they said and did. We wanted them to know the blessing of staying on God's "path of life." When they strayed off the path, we used the ways to gently guide them back. The ways helped us talk about the importance of making wise decisions, and the associated scripture helped us talk about God's heart and following the wisdom of His Word to stay on the "way of life." However, the Ways are not just rules to follow and obey, but language that will help your children learn and internalize biblical family values. They were for giving our children the words to say what we, and they, believe.

Make your own ways: As a family, decide what your "ways" will be—identify the scriptures that best express your convictions, and then make a list of simple statements that define the attitudes and behaviors you want to practice in your home. These statements will become the language of biblical family values that define your family. They are not laws to keep or break, but ways to shape and direct you and your children in the way of God's wisdom.

Don't Neglect to Confront Sin

Just do it: Confronting a child's sin is one of my least favorite things to do. I love harmony and I love to be close to my children, but not at the expense of neglecting or ignoring sin or misbehavior. Not exercising discipline is still a form of discipline, but it teaches the wrong thing. If I let a child's complaining or ungraciousness or whining go unchecked, and undisciplined, I would be training them to weakness, teaching them that sin has no consequence. I confront those sins out of love that wants them to know God's forgiveness and blessings for obedience and wisdom. "If we confess our sins, He is faithful and righteous to forgive us our sins and to cleanse us from all unrighteousness" (1 John 1:9).

Talk about it: When your children struggle with an attitude or action you see as being sinful, talk with them about it first. The first response to sin should always be verbal discipline—confronting the problem with love and firmness, explaining why it is sinful or not wise, discussing with them what God says in His Word about it, defining the choice that needs to be made, and encouraging them to change. In essence, verbal discipline creates the opportunity for confession and repentance. Have the child memorize a verse that speaks to their behavior, and let them know you have confidence in them to overcome the sin and please God in the future. Don't become weary—keep training, keep loving, and keep confronting

Create Habits of Character at Home

Housework and chores build character: The ever-present reality of keeping a house clean and orderly, with a disorder-producing family living in it, is a natural training ground for character development of children. From the time our children were little, we assigned chores and trained them (slowly but surely) to diligence, responsibility, and faithfulness. The habits we tried to instill early on were the beginnings of *Our 24 Family Ways*. Training habits for household chores is where foundational character habits are formed in children. Hold your children accountable not just for doing their chores, but also for doing them with the proper attitude. This is where the Our 24 Family Ways come in handy: "We are diligent to complete a task promptly and thoroughly when asked" (Way 13), and "We take initiative to do all of our own work without needing to be told" (Way 14).

Family devotions reinforce character training: A regular family devotion every day will help to reinforce the character habits you are training in your children. If you consider your family devotional—reading God's Word, talking about it, praying—a sacred time for your family, it will reinforce the importance of God's Word for your children when you use it in your discipline and training. If you don't have a devotional planned, just pick a good verse or passage and use the family devotional **ARTS** outline—**A**sk a question; **R**ead the Bible; **T**alk about It: **S**peak to God.

Personal devotions build character: Training your children to have a regular, daily "quiet time" or personal devotional also trains their character. First, it trains your children to a habit. A habit of devotion not only influences your children spiritually, it is also positive practice for other habits of character. Second, a regular time with God creates a sense of inner accountability, not just to the habit itself, but to God who is the object of that habit. Finally, the more they learn how to listen to God, the more seriously they will learn to consider their responsibilities as a Christian child. It's all interconnected.

Provide Literary Models of Character

Read good moral stories: There are many collections of short "moral stories" available from the past two centuries. The older ones can sometimes veer a bit too much into legalism, but they are mostly stories about choosing God's ways over the world's ways, with good examples of moral character, excellence, and virtue in children that are great for discussion. Though some may seem old-fashioned now (innocence and purity are not popular for modern children), they offer living pictures of character that you can adapt to your own culture and family. Some of the best known collections include: "Uncle Arthur's Bedtime Stories" (numerous volumes); *Tiger and Tom and Other Stories for Boys*, and *The King's Daughter and Other Stories for Girls*; *A Young Person's Guide to Knowing God* (Patricia St. John); and many others.

Read good children's literature: The Victorian era of the late nineteenth century created the enriched cultural soil in which "The Golden Age" of children's literature took root and grew. In the expanding world of publishing, children became a "market" for the first time, and the high regard in that era for duty, honor, nobility, and virtue is reflected in much of what we now call classic children's literature. You can find many excellent literary examples of character to imprint in your children's imaginations by reading good stories. To find the best ones, look in Sarah's book *Read for the Heart – Whole Books for WholeHearted Families*.

Speak Vision into Their Lives

Say what you see for them: Inspiration and vision are key words in the development of character. As you train your children, make sure you're always looking for times to articulate your vision of what you hope they will become. In other words, speak into their minds and hearts pictures of the virtue, honor, and character that can make them a great person in history, and even more, in God's eyes. Also speak biblical truths to your children that you can personalize for them. Remind them of who they are as children of God, and all the things God has already done for them, and will do for them. Put their name into a Scripture passage. Many parents who never experienced this kind of language growing up from their parents, will need to learn and practice it in order to make it a natural part of their own parenting. It is worth the effort, though. It will change your children's live, and maybe even your own life.

Affirm what you see in them: A simple affirmation may be a seed for future aspiration: "You were so noble and brave when you spoke up for your friend when others were making fun of her. It makes me so proud, and I can see the kind of man you will one day become." Affirmation should not be confused with flattery. When you affirm your child's character or choices, you're telling them something true about themselves, and letting them know why it is admirable and good. Affirming character is like commenting on what makes a painting or a song beautiful. It's a limited expression of why a part of your child's character is noteworthy and worthy of affirmation.

Assign Historical Character Studies

Have your children pick their favorite historical figures, and show them how to do a character study of that person—writing about the habits, qualities, attitudes, and actions that made that person great (as well as what may have been not so great things about their life). When Nathan was nine, he did a character study of Audie Murphy, a WWII hero, and then gave a presentation to a group of friends on Murphy's courage in battle, his initiative and ingenuity when faced with problems, his perseverance when all hope seemed lost, and his good attitude throughout. Nathan beamed as he gave that speech, and I knew at the end of it that he had a new idea of excellence for himself. Gather biographies, movies, audiodrama, and books to help your child to get well acquainted with the habits of heroes.

Serve in Your Community and Church

Having the accountability and encouragement of friends and mentors can be a huge incentive to help children learn to become excellent. We found ways to get our children involved in helping out with a Sunday school, putting shoeboxes of gifts together at Christmas time, volunteering at a homeless shelter, or simply cleaning the house of a neighbor or friend. The accountability of having other adults encouraging them to work hard and to serve well helped our children see themselves as members of and contributors to the wider community. Character training is, in many ways, about giving your child an identity as a trustworthy person. Community can contribute to this in a powerful and positive way.

❤

Wrapping Up the Gift

I will give my child a heart for Character by:

_____

_____

_____

_____

_____

_____

_____

_____

_____

_____

_____

_____

_____

_____

_____

_____

He who loves purity of **heart**
and whose speech is gracious,
the king is his friend.

— PROVERBS 22:11 —

CHAPTER 4

A HEART FOR MANNERS

The Gift of a Gracious Presence

*Let your speech always be with grace, as though
seasoned with salt, so that you will know how you
should respond to each person.*

COLOSSIANS 4:6

*Life is short, but there is always time enough for
courtesy.*

RALPH WALDO EMERSON

Often I wondered if my children were listening to everything I taught them. Their progress in life and godliness sometimes felt painfully slow, especially when it came to manners. Nathan, my very extroverted child, was a particular challenge. He disliked rules and was prone to say whatever came to his mind. No matter how hard I sought to give him a sense of honor for others and a grid of graciousness through which to relate to all people, I wondered if my instruction was really taking root.

One summer, Nate was invited to spend several weeks by himself at a friend's home. He was deeply excited, as this presented an adventure all his own and would also be the first time he had flown on an airplane by himself. With a dozen motherly admonitions, I sent him off and told him to be sure to call me when he arrived safely. My phone rang that evening and as I answered, his excited voice bubbled over through the receiver.

"Hey, Mama. It was so much fun to fly by myself. And you will never believe what happened! The stewardess talked to me during the whole flight because I had a seat at the front. I remembered to ask her questions instead of doing all the talking. I thanked her when she served me. I told her I appreciated her helping me when I was looking for my seat. She said, 'You know, Nathan, you are one of the most polite boys I have met in a long time. It was really a pleasure having you on my plane!'

Can you believe she said that about me, Mom? I felt just like I was an adult!"

When I recovered from my shock, I smiled and congratulated him as heartily as I could. In the midst of that proud mama moment, I realized that all of those minutes, hours, days, weeks, and years of hard work and training had truly paid off. After all of those times when I wondered if Nathan was listening, I realized that he had taken it in after all. He actually knew how to be polite! Renewed in my resolve, I kept on with my training, and Nathan was ready for more when he got home.

❤

Manners are essential to anyone who wants to lead or succeed in the world. A person who can speak with confidence, greet new acquaintances with poise, converse with grace, and even know how to comport oneself at a social dinner, has a set of skills that will enable them to be a presence of grace in any setting in the world. They will be able to "become all things to all people" (1 Corinthians 9:22b, NIV) as Paul said of his own ministry, or as Kipling expressed in his poem "If", they would be able "to talk with crowds and keep your virtue, or walk with Kings—nor lose the common touch." We no longer live in an age that values manners as they once were. They are seen more as old-fashioned rules, or a set of silly social behaviors. But that misses what I believe is the real and critical value of manners in any time—they are a way of extending grace to every person you meet.

Manners are not about "me," but about others. At their heart, manners are about the social and spiritual poise that enables one to become skilled in relating to other people in any situation—setting them at ease, maintaining a sense of social confidence, and exercising self-control in any situation. Manners are graciousness in action—the extension of grace to others that makes them feel noticed, accepted, and affirmed. Just as God's grace does for us.

Even common, every day table manners are important. When you teach your child to sit up straight, keep their mouth closed when chewing, and use a napkin instead of their sleeve, you are actually giving them the ability to influence others. A lack of good manners can easily become a barrier to being able to extend grace to others, a closed door. Good manners, on the other hand, keep doors and windows of relationship open.

When you show your child how to shake an adult's hand firmly, look a person in the eye and greet them with respect, and speak to a stranger or new acquaintance confidently and winsomely, you are instructing your children in the art of graciousness—showing respect and honor to others. When you teach them poise—how to stand still without fidgeting, or how to handle awkward people—you are giving them an inner strength that will serve them in every new job, home, or country they encounter.

In our increasingly casual, coarse, and common world, many mothers despair of teaching their children good manners. It's one thing to teach them "Yes mam ... No mam ... Thank you ... Please," and being polite and quiet, but the manners that will matter will require more training. Children don't take to manners naturally, as Nathan (and all of my children) so often proved. However, I believe that training a child to have good manners can help to shape the kind of person they become and influence the kind of life they will live.

Just as ambassadors are trained to relate to all manner of people in all kinds of situations, and to engage in reconciling disagreements between people of different cultures, manners will enable your child to be an ambassador for the values and virtues of Christ you have instilled into them. Manners equip them to engage with confidence in any social setting or relational situation in which God puts them, and to be a winsome witness for Him simply by their presence, and by knowing how to behave properly and relate well to others.

The book of Proverbs is full of practical wisdom, including social skills for a variety of situations. When Solomon says, "Train up a child in the way he should go, even when he is old he will not depart from it" (Proverbs 22:6), that "way" encompasses everything that makes a well-rounded person. All training, whether spiritual or practical, is a continuous, daily process of forming new habits.

Every new acquaintance, every mealtime, every interaction with an adult is an occasion through which you can train your child's manners. At first, you may wonder if any of it is taking hold at all, but it is. Keep on saying the same things again and again—"Don't talk with food in your mouth!" and "Hold the door open for your sister!" and "Go introduce yourself to our guests." Your ongoing training is never wasted.

Always keep in mind, though, in the midst of training your children in manners, what the real goal of it all really is—being faithful stewards of God's love. Your children need to know that more than just being well-behaved or socially confident or mannerly, good manners can be a way for them to love others. That's the way we, as believers, should think about learning them. Not just as rules of etiquette, but as a way to fulfill Christ's commandment to love others as we love God and ourselves.

As followers of God, we are showing the world what He is like with every word and action. Manners are just one more way of communicating God's love and kindness, showing honor and respect, conferring dignity and value, and above all offering grace. In the words of Elsa Maxwell, "Etiquette—a fancy word for simple kindness." Or, expressed in another way, "Good manners—a simple way for showing God's love." Good manners are channels through which God is showing His love to others through us.

❤

GIVING THE GIFT OF MANNERS

Start with the Basics

There are countless books on etiquette. When I was training my children, I looked through quite a few manners manuals to gain a vision for the social skills I wanted to instill in them. The list I created became my training guide. The following is just a tiny sampler, and you can add many more of your own, but following are some examples of where to begin training.

Table manners: My children needed to learn, among many other things, the proper use of silverware, to put their napkin in their lap, chew with mouth closed, keep elbows off the table and hands in their laps, and wait for the hostess to take the first bite.

Meet and greet: First impressions are more powerful than we like to admit. I was adamant that my children know how to firmly grasp and shake an adult's hand, and to look an adult or new acquaintance in the eyes and introduce themselves with poise. It was also important to me that they know how to address their elders with respect.

Conversation: Being a good conversationalist consists mostly of listening, asking good questions, and giving thoughtful answers. I wanted my children to be responsible to take initiative to talk with other people—to engage others in conversation and to communicate interest their lives. This also includes things such as knowing not to interrupt others (especially an adult), how to politely excuse yourself from a conversation, how to show attentiveness, and even how to graciously respond to inappropriate talk (ethnic jokes, criticism of others, etc.).

Hosting: A good host or hostess can set the tone of their home for a visitor just by their demeanor and welcome. I wanted my children to learn how to welcome and greet guests with grace and confidence, offer refreshment and direct them where to go, and introduce them to other guests. Good hosting is also being aware of guest's needs throughout their visit.

Composure: In every situation, regardless of their impatience or irritation, I wanted my children to learn the discipline of being composed and poised in public. That meant practicing self-control of emotions and body language. It meant controlling frustration and anger. It meant overcoming fear and anxiety to give a short speech or meet a new person. Exercising composure and poise is a discipline of the spirit that must be learned.

Honor: Perhaps beyond all the manners and skills, I wanted my children to learn that they should always honor adults and show a respectful attitude toward authority. All of my children are generally strong-willed, so I knew it was important to cultivate an attitude of humility in them and to help them understand that honoring elders is part of honoring God.

Practice in Real Life

One of the most beneficial aspects of learning social skills is the confidence they enable you to feel in any situation. Encourage your children and provide an outlet for them to practice these skills by creating familiar circumstances for them to try them out.

Eating out: Plan a special meal, and use it for rehearsing manners and skills. Take your daughter(s) out for a dress-up ladies lunch. Encourage them to look at the menu and order for themselves, which will enable them to practice speaking as and to an adult when ordering. Go through basic etiquette with them—putting their napkin in their lap, praying before the meal, chewing with mouth closed, not talking while chewing, and keeping their voice down while in a public place. This doesn't have to be an expensive event; my little ladies have fond memories of practicing these skills even over sandwiches and French fries. You, and your husband, can do the same with your boys, choosing a restaurant they will enjoy but rehearsing the same manners. Or, you can take all your children, girls and boys, out and "test" them on their manners knowledge.

On the phone: Phone calls are an excellent way for your children to practice speaking confidently to adults. Teach them how to properly answer a phone call—"Hello. This is Sarah speaking." Discuss what kinds of questions they should ask the person on the line—"How are you? How is your day going? What have you been doing lately?" Role-play phone calls for practice. For instance, pretend that you are "Grandma" calling and have your child rehearse answering the call, and engaging in confident, polite conversation.

Talking with adults: The entire time I was raising my four children, our home was often filled with guests. This was a wonderful opportunity for them to get first-hand learning experience in conversing with adults. Carrying on conversations with grown-ups can be extremely intimidating, especially for children who are naturally more shy and introverted. Encourage your children to speak with the adults in your home; don't just let your children disappear to their rooms. The more practice your children get, the better.

Asking questions: Teach your children to be people who initiate and ask questions. Asking thoughtful questions and being a great listener—being genuinely interested, authentic, and engaged in another person's thoughts—will capture the attention and hearts of others and set your children apart. Showing interest in someone else's stories affirms them as a person worthy of attention, an act of love. And by knowing how to keep the conversation flowing and fill the gaps of silence, you put the other person at ease, an act of grace. Practice this with your children on a regular basis, and prepare them before any family outing by asking what questions they will ask their friends or new people they might meet.

Politeness: Always remind your children that "polite" is a state of mind—it is a choice to practice politeness by drawing from the well of everything you know about manners for whatever situation you find yourself. Talk to them about polite conversation (asking questions, complimenting, making small talk, telling about a new hobby), polite behavior (shaking hands, opening doors, pulling out seats), and polite table manners. Everything is open for discussion under the politeness policy of your family. Be sure also to talk about what is NOT polite discussion (gossip, off-color topics, criticism, personal information about your family).

Role-play: Practice different potential situations with your children before social events or guests come over. Role-play and allow them to practice how they will greet guests, talk with an adult, and respond to questions so that they feel comfortable and confident in those circumstances rather than quietly hiding behind you.

Prepare: If your family is going to a party or event where there will be other adults, take the time to do some manners reinforcement and practice. Use the "Thumbs Up ... Thumbs Down" game to review proper behavior. For instance, you say: "When you meet the host, should you immediately ask where the toys are?" Everyone calls out a big "Noooo!" and gives a thumbs down. "When you get dessert, should you take one or two things, or all that you want?" They respond by loudly repeating "one or two things" with a thumbs up. You can show different facial expressions and body language to which they will respond with thumbs up or down. Let them suggest scenarios that are on their mind and do the same. It's a fun way to remind and reinforce some basic manners that you want them to remember.

The Importance of Body Language

Studies suggest that over 90% of our communication is nonverbal—facial expressions, movements, body posture, use of hands and arms, head movements. In other words, we can say more by what we don't say than by what we do say. If most interpersonal communication is nonverbal, then we need to be sure our children understand the language of the body and how to use it, or not use it.

Learn positive body language: Body language used positively can communicate interest, engagement, respect, affection, agreement, and much more. When speaking, body language can also add emphasis, conviction, concern, and excitement to your words. Body language can also communicate, intentionally or unintentionally, disinterest, disagreement, boredom, disdain, and other negative nonverbal messages. Train your children that what they show is ultimately just as or more important that what they say.

Rehearse to remember: Practice communicating nonverbally with one another using body language. First, call out familiar attitudes and emotions, and have your children show each one nonverbally—interested, nervous, excited, bored, friendly. Then, have your children choose an attitude secretly, show it with body language, and you guess what they are "saying." Have your child tell a story, or something that happened in their day that is really important to them. While they are speaking, tap your foot, wiggle around, yawn, and cross your arms. Then, tell your child to start over. This time, look at your child, engage in the conversation, nod your head in agreement, and smile. Talk to your child about how they felt about what you were saying nonverbally each time.

Engage with confidence: Encourage your children to look others in the eyes when they are speaking to them. This is not only polite, but also lets the speaker know that you are truly interested in what they have to say. Many shy, introverted children struggle with this due to a lack of confidence. Studies have shown that darting of the eyes, looking away, or closing the eyes is a subconscious blocking behavior to cope with feelings of intimidation, anxiety, and insecurity. Practice making eye contact and conversation together in a nonthreatening place and way. As your child becomes more comfortable with eye contact and speaking, it will boost their self-esteem, and strengthen their confidence for using those skills in real life.

Don't fidget: Moving around and fidgeting is our body's natural way of dealing with stress, insecurity, and anxiety. Help your children learn to breathe deeply, to be aware of their movement, and to fix their attention on the person before them. Talk to your children about what certain body movements might communicate negatively to others—shoulder shrugs make us look disinterested, fidgeting says "I'm bored," tapping feet suggests nervousness, looking away communicates a desire to be somewhere else, crossed arms and yawning is just rude neglect. Once you explain these, then expect your children to avoid them in public.

♥

Wrapping Up the Gift

I will give my child a heart for Manners by:

_____

_____

_____

_____

_____

_____

_____

_____

_____

_____

_____

_____

_____

_____

_____

Obey them not only to win their favor when
their eye is on you, but like slaves of Christ,
doing the will of God from your **heart.**

— EPHESIANS 6:6 NIV —

— CHAPTER 5 —

A HEART FOR SERVICE
The Gift of Giving Yourself

For even the Son of Man did not come to be served, but to serve, and to give His life a ransom for many.

MARK 10:45

Make it a rule, and pray to God to help you to keep it, never, if possible, to lie down at night without being able to say: "I have made one human being at least a little wiser, or a little happier, or at least a little better this day.

CHARLES KINGSLEY

Even though the rain slowed me down, my heart was in a hurry as we pulled up to a stoplight in Nashville. That's when we all saw the weather-beaten man on the curb holding up a rain-soaked sign. It was just Joel, 7, and Nathan, 5, in the backseat, and we were running late for their weekly music lessons. My anxious heart thumped to the rhythm of the windshield wipers as I waited for the green light to go. I quickly glanced at the bedraggled figure standing outside our car. No. I couldn't stop today. Not today. There simply wasn't time.

"Mama," Nathan's voice piped up from the backseat. "Look at that man in the rain. Look, he has a sign. He must be cold."

Then Joel joined in to read the words off the soaked sign: "'Homeless. Anything helps. God bless.'" I was still looking at the light waiting for green. "Look, Mom, he only has one leg."

For a moment, Joel contemplated this observation with a solemn, sad little face, and then he turned to me, eyes big and urgent. I knew where this was headed.

"Mom, we should help him. We should buy him a hamburger!" I glanced at my watch and scouted the busy street for any nearby fast food restaurants. There were none in sight. But Joel, seeing the hesitation in my face, leaned forward from the back, straining against his seatbelt. "Come on, Mom," he urged, "he really needs our help, and you've told us we should always try to help the people God puts in our way."

He was right. Clay and I were always telling our kids to keep their eyes open for the people God might put in their lives who needed their help or kindness. We wanted our kids to see themselves as servants, to have a self-perception as givers. I couldn't argue with Joel's impulse to give. I decided that today music lessons would simply have to wait and I rolled down my window.

"Hello, sir," I said as the man moved stiffly toward us. "My boys want to buy you some lunch."

Before he could say anything, Joel interjected, "Ask him if he wants hamburger or chicken." Nathan added his own high-pitched command to be sure to find out his favorite drink. The man told me what he liked and we took off as the light finally turned green.

By the time we found a McDonald's, ordered the food (with many directions from my boys—"Supersize it, Mom, he looks really hungry!"), and made it back to the stoplight, the rain had lifted a little and the man shuffled over to meet us. As I handed him the bag of hot food and the supersized soft drink, the boys piped up from the back, "We got you a hamburger like you said, and lots of French fries!" The man took the food, then put his hands on the window and leaned into the car.

"Boys," he said looking back at each of them, "thank you so much. You're the first people who have stopped all day. What are your names?" The boys told him, and the man nodded, "Well, thank you Joel, and thank you Nathan. God bless you."

"What's your name?" piped up Nathan from the back as the man turned to go.

"Michael," he said simply, and with a nod to me, walked away as we drove away.

That night, as I put Nathan to bed and prepared to pray for him, he looked up at me with a very serious face. "Let's pray for Michael, Mama," he said, and that began a month in which the boys prayed every night fervently for Michael, "our homeless man."

As I watched their little hearts ache for the loneliness and hurt of another person, I thanked God that I had taken the time to stop, to live out the message I was trying so hard to teach them every day in our home: how to have the heart of a giver, the heart of a servant.

❤

From the time our kids were old enough to listen, Clay and I told them over and over, "I wonder how God will use you in the world—whose heart you will heal or what truth you will bring." We wanted our children to think of themselves, even when they were little, as those who had a responsibility to be generous in giving and loving as they served others. One of the main goals of our training was for our children to leave our home with a sense of personal mission—the conviction that they were called to be the hands and feet of Christ in the world. Clay and I both came to marriage with a background in ministry, so this was part of our identity and vision for our family from the beginning.

But the model that drove the training of our children didn't come simply from our backgrounds, but from our study of Christ and His kingdom. Our ultimate goal was to raise children who walked closely with God, who knew His love, and who brought His kingdom to bear on earth. The cultivation of a servant's heart in our children was simply one of the most vital ways to connect them to the reality of the gospel, to help them understand their lives as part of God's story.

But we live in a "me" culture of consumption and distraction that says to children and young adults, and to parents, that happiness in life is about having, not giving. Even good Christian parents, acting with good intentions, can get caught up in that cultural spirit—spending so much time and money giving their children great experiences, keeping up with cultural trends and fads so their children will "fit in," giving them all the best things to make home the place they will want to be.

Even good parents, thinking they're doing good, can make their children self-centered, growing up with the expectation that what they've known is how the real world really works. Those children might never get the truth down into their hearts that their lives, and the love and blessing they have known and received, are a gift from God to be given to others. The real world is not about having, but about giving.

Teaching what it means to have a servant's heart is a radical departure from the way of the world. It is teaching your children the way of Christ, who gave up His life so that we could know His love and grace. Training your children to have a servant's heart isn't about completing a list of service projects or giving a certain amount of money; it's about giving your children the core identity and self-image of a giver, a servant. They need to know that they are called to follow in the footsteps of the God whose kingdom story they are called to live and share. As I worked to create this identity in my children,

I learned that there is a process by which such a self-image is formed. Let's call it the "work in process."

The first part of that "work in process" was modeling—it all starts with me as a mother. Before my children could embrace the sacrifices of servanthood, they needed to see their mama do it first. I quickly learned that my attitudes about work, my moods as I cleaned or cooked, my joy (or lack of it) when company came, all were immediately communicated to my children. Their attitudes were a mirror of mine. If I complained, they complained. If I was critical, they were critical.

I always found that the best way I could teach my children how to serve with a willing and joyous heart was simply to do it myself—to be a model of the kind of attitude I wanted them to learn. And I found that when I took the time to serve them personally, their hearts softened and they were willing to listen to my training.

Joy, my youngest child, has always responded to gifts of service. I am not a detail-oriented person, so I don't always think of these things, but one year, when we were going to be out of town a lot, I had the idea of helping Joy pack her suitcase, something she usually did on her own. She had seemed particularly moody and unhelpful in the previous few days, but I just sat on the floor in her room, helped her select outfits and shoes, and fit them all into her suitcase with her. The longer we sat, the chattier she got, and I watched her countenance soften. When I stood up at the end, she hugged me and said, "Thanks for serving me, Mama. I know you're busy, but it means a lot to me."

Your children will never know what it means to serve in love—to truly offer their time, their lives, and their resources to others—unless they experience it first in their own home, and from their own parents.

The second part of the "work in process" was companionship—having my children serve alongside me. Clay and I involved the kids in almost every aspect of our ministry from the start. Sarah and Joel sealed envelopes and stamped newsletters; all of them babysat kids of the parents we counseled; they served at conferences, and carried suitcases for the moms who came to our ministry events. "If it is God's will for us to be in ministry, it's God's will for you to be, too," we said. We started every conference with an evening of training for our kids and the volunteers, talking about why we ministered and what kind of heart we wanted them to have for our guests.

When we traveled, the kids often had to sleep on makeshift beds on the floor or watch the younger children of host families as ministry events were going on. At home, several of my mom friends and I arranged for our kids to sing and perform a short drama for the residents of a nearby nursing home. My boys worked several days each Christmas with a shoebox ministry. By involving our children in every aspect of ministry and seeking out opportunities for them to serve at home, we hoped to pass on our own vision for our family and ourselves as servants in God's kingdom.

But we also cultivated a culture of servanthood with one another. It's far easier to serve a stranger than a sibling, so we worked hard to create a culture of kindness in our home. When one child was having a hard day, we encouraged the others to make their sibling a cup of tea, take over a chore, or even just give them a few kind words. We trained them to speak graciously and to serve one another by refraining from criticism or harshness. We trained them to be givers, not only to the world, but also to each other.

The third part of the "work in process" was spontaneity—being ready to give and serve whenever God brings an opportunity into your life, like with Michael, the boys' "homeless man." Cultivating a heart of spontaneous service in your children can be a lot of fun, if everyone is ready to "go where the Spirit leads."

When faced with a blue day, one of our children spontaneously said, "Let's make dozens of cookies and surprise every friend we love and take all afternoon to deliver cookies and tell everyone how much we appreciate them!" Soon all our "woe is me" attitudes were turned into "giving is fun!" attitudes. It was such a delight to get everyone involved. Even little three-year-old Joy caught the spirit and helped. It took us all day, but we took cookies to everyone. And as a result, many of our friends ended up asking us over for lunch, meeting us at the park, and telling us how very much our love gift meant to them. To this day, my children bake something, make "I love you" flower bouquets, or create a special card to give to those they love as a surprise.

The final "work in process" was equipping—giving our children skills and encouragement to give and serve in their own unique ways. This was an exciting process as we sat down with each of them once they were old enough and asked them what God had put on their hearts to do for other people. Their answers were as diverse as their personalities. Sarah wrote letters to several lonely elderly women. Joel gave all of the coins he had saved for a year to a homeless shelter. Nathan did magic tricks for a group of little kids. Joy volunteered to mentor young girls. We helped them to gather whatever they needed, we encouraged, we prayed, and then we let them give. I will never forget the glow on Joel's face when he gave his money to the shelter.

"Mom," he said, "I think it really helped them." So it did. But it also helped him to see himself as a giver, and that is a gift I hope he carries with him all his days.

❤

GIVING THE GIFT OF SERVICE

Serve in a Variety of Ways

Serving is more than just working, or helping others. Training your children to serve can encompass a wide variety of activities—speaking truth to seekers, comforting the hurting, giving to needs and causes, loving the unloved and unlovely, even creating a tool or device that will help others. Consider how your own family, with your own unique set of gifts and personalities, could serve the world of needs around you. Be creative, be bold, have fun. Some of our best memories as a family center around the times we served other people together. Here are a few idea starters for service:

Serving your neighbor: Look for hands-on jobs that you and your children could do together to serve a neighbor—yardwork, snow removal, watching their pets, cooking a meal, picking up mail when gone, help with housework. Elderly widows are especially in need of assistance, and even just a nice visit. Not only will it teach your children service, it will also build bridges of relationship in your neighborhood.

Serving with hospitality: The art of hospitality is a service that, once learned, will stick with your children for life. It's also one of the most enjoyable ways to serve others as a family. Make a habit of hospitality in your home by inviting families over for a meal. Let your children help with all the preparations, cleaning, cooking, decorating, lighting candles, and arranging flowers. Teach them to understand that the preparation of the house and the giving of the meal is a way of showing love to those who come.

Serving your church and community: Volunteering to help with projects at your church is an easy and manageable way for you and your children to practice serving. Every church is always shorthanded for some task or ministry and will be grateful to see a family coming to help. Community projects often have sufficient volunteers, but it's a great way to get to know others outside your Christian fellowship circles, most of whom will be of other faiths and nonbelievers, and be a part of helping with something that will help others in your wider community.

Serving by giving: Training your children to become cheerful and generous givers will enable them to serve others close to them, or well beyond their reach. When they are young, encourage them to be generous to meet the needs of others they know or see in your church or community. When they are older, entrust them with some funds to steward by choosing where to give it. Help them set aside part of their own money to give. Giving is a service to God.

Serving by sponsoring: There are numerous wonderful Christian aid programs, such as Compassion and World Vision, through which you can sponsor a child overseas. Take some time to choose an area of the world to help, review children available to sponsor, pray about the choices, and select one or more children together as a family to sponsor. Schedule regular times to meet together at home to pray for your child, write letters to them, and send monetary gifts. As your children get older, challenge them to earn extra money to sponsor their own child.

Serving spontaneously: The hardest obstacle to overcome in serving others is when you're faced with a need or an opportunity to serve, but your life is already planned and scheduled. Learning how to be spontaneous in serving is an attitude and discipline. It's not always possible to serve, of course, but the heart of "find a way" to serve is, perhaps, closer to serving as Jesus served. Just like the boys and "their homeless man" or the afternoon cookie episode, spontaneity is arguably the truest test of a heart to serve. As a parent, though, if you train your children to look for spontaneous opportunities to serve or help, always be ready to say "Yes" if you're able when they, like my boys did, want to act.

Serving by teaching: Sarah is my introverted girl, but I knew she had a lot of wisdom and love she could share with young girls. So I challenged her to put together a talk and begin a small Bible study. She was a little overwhelmed at first, but when she shared what she had learned in her quiet time and watched the girls respond, she glowed. "I think God really used me to tell them something," she beamed. We believe that God has put a message in the heart of every child, and it is part of a parent's role to help them identify it and use it to serve others.

- What messages do your children have within them? What truth do they know? What truth needs to be spoken into our culture today? What are they passionate about? Help your children identify ideas they are passionate about, find an audience they can speak or write to, and craft a message of influence or inspiration.

- Who could your children mentor? Once you know truth, you become a steward of it. One of my best friends says all discipleship should be up and down; in other words, you should have someone above you as a mentor, and below you as a disciple. Are there friends or even siblings that your own children could teach? Challenge them to serve by their influence and words.

Serve Others with Friends

Serving alone misses the blessings of shared service. Find a way to serve with others from your church, a fellowship group, or even your local community. The joy that comes when many people work together on a project or task is something that could deeply impact your children and will help them to feel part of a fellowship in which everyone serves. Think about the shared pride that comes with being part of a team building a Habit for Humanity home. Or, of when teams from your church set aside Saturdays to go into distressed neighborhoods to help with home upkeep and repair, and yard work and cleanup. Working in ministry (service) is meant to be done together as the people of God.

Family projects: Get several families together and have the kids learn several songs or put together a short drama to offer at a local retirement or nursing home. My children did this with friends for many years and still love to remember the way the residents smiled, sang along, and sometimes even cried.

Teen crews: Round up a gang of your older kids and challenge them to take on somebody's yard work for a day. Or, to paint a home in a needy area with your church. Or, clean up a stretch of highway in your town. Make a great picnic and praise them to the skies for all they get done.

Poundings: Have a "pounding" for new neighbors or for friends who will be moving into a new house. It's an old term for stocking a kitchen with a "pound" of the necessaries—canned goods, paper products, flour, sugar, condiments, and all the rest. Make it a group project. Bring pizza and drinks to welcome them in on their first day in the house.

Seek Out Role Models of Service

A heart for service is arguably more caught than taught. Your children will catch a heart for serving primarily from your home, but also from many other sources, some as primary influences and others as reinforcing influences. You will always be the first primary influence, but all the role models and messages you can put into your child's life will help build in them a heart to serve.

Bible: Direct your children into a study of biblical characters who were servants. Have each child choose someone specific, such as David, who tended his father's sheep; or Ruth, who worked in the fields; or Mary, who was a bondservant of the Lord; or Jesus, who washed the disciples' feet. Have them describe how their biblical hero served others and what their kind of service says about their character.

Books: Read biographies together of historical men and women who served others. Talk about them, and how to emulate their service even in a small way. Read great children's literature and classic novels that provide literary models of characters known for their service and sacrifice. Talk about what can be learned even from a fictional account of serving.

People: Observe and learn about people in the news who are known for their service or sacrifice on behalf of others. Find stories and documentary videos of real people today who are serving others. Talk about real examples of service as a family and what you can learn and emulate from them.

Ministries and Charities: Identify and learn more about local nonprofit ministries and charities that are serving specific needs and people groups in your city or community. Talk with the founders to hear their hearts for service. Get involved as a family in a ministry or charity that is helping in ways that resonate with your own beliefs and convictions.

Missionaries: Read about missionaries who are serving people in other countries. Talk about how they are serving to help others have better lives. Discuss what makes them different, what motivates them to sacrifice their own lives for the benefit of others, and how you can learn from their examples.

Friends: Find ways for your children to spend time with family or church friends they admire and who have a heart for service. One of my dearest friends gives health and nutrition classes and lets teenage girls assist her with the kitchen work. Sharing a morning or a day with a special person in an act of service can have a lasting impact on your children's attitudes about serving.

Mentors: Seek out mentors in ministry who will agree to meet with your child regularly to influence them spiritually. Let them accompany the mentor in their occupation or ministry of service. A friend of mine works with foster kids and trains teenagers how to be mentors to kids from broken homes. A mentor can be a powerful testimony of service, as well as a teacher and influencer of a child's faith and convictions.

❤

Wrapping Up the Gift

I will give my child a heart for Service by:

_____

_____

_____

_____

_____

_____

_____

_____

_____

_____

_____

_____

_____

_____

May he give you the desire of your **heart**
and make all your plans succeed.

— PSALM 20:4 NIV —

CHAPTER 6

A HEART FOR WORK

The Gift of Purposeful Industry

*[M]ake it your ambition to lead a quiet life and attend
to your own business and work with your hands, just
as we commanded you, so that you will behave
properly toward outsiders and not be in any need.*

1 THESSALONIANS 4:11-12

*Teaching children the joy of honest labor is one of the
greatest of all gifts you can bestow upon them.*

L. TOM PERRY

In the early years of our ministry, when we were in Texas still getting everything off the ground, there was a time when our home and our ministry offices were an hour apart. It was not unusual for our whole family to spend several days away from home for a speaking or exhibiting event, and then as soon as we got back Clay would have to leave to spend several days away at the office. We worked hard, and worked to make our situation work. It was not an easy time.

When it was just me at home without Clay, the extra work often left me worn out. I remember one time trying to manage my four children, cooking, teaching, and giving Joy her middle of the night asthma treatments had left me especially ragged and exhausted. In the midst of the tumult, Sarah, newly thirteen but older than her age, came into the den as I was straightening up from a very busy day.

"Mama," she said, "we kids have a favor to ask you. Would you mind going to the store to get some ice cream so we can have a fun night together? We have a little surprise for you."

Unable to bear the thought of disappointing my bright-eyed, expectant children, I agreed to their request with a tired compliance. I wearily climbed into my car and drove to the store. I got the requested ice cream, and a few other groceries, and returned home about an hour later. By the time I reached the front porch, weariness was a weight on my shoulders. I opened door and stumbled in. And stopped.

The familiar messy den I had left an hour before had been transformed. Candles were lit. Music was on. All was perfectly in order. I continued on through the house. Dishes and pans in the kitchen sink had been washed and put away. Two baskets of laundry had been folded and distributed. And when I looked in my bedroom, the sheets on my bed were turned down and a cup of tea was on my bedside table. And on the pillow there was a note from all the children, with even a few scratchy letters from three-year-old Joy. I read the heartwarming note:

Dear Mama,

We know you are tired without having Daddy home. But we wanted you to know how much we love you and appreciate you. Let's have a fun night and you can even go to sleep early and we will put ourselves in bed.

Love,
Your Children

Sarah, of course, as the oldest child, was the instigator. But all the kids had pitched in to give this gift to their mama. They had all grown up helping me daily with the chores. They knew how much work a family like ours required, and how much it would mean to me that they had taken the initiative to work on their own. Their surprise was an even greater gift to me than they knew because it showed me that they were beginning to see themselves as capable workers in our home.

❤

From the time my children could do chores, they heard mom talk about work. I knew that one of the most vital qualities I could pass on to them would be a good attitude about work. A healthy, biblical attitude about work would influence their chosen vocation in life, their relationships with authorities, and even the harmony of their own future homes and families.

A good work ethic is central to a whole and well-rounded life; embracing work, in whatever form it would take in their lives, would enable my children to flourish as adults. The apostle Paul said it clearly: "Whatever you do, do your work heartily, as for the Lord, rather than for men" (Colossians 3:23). Working heartily at whatever they do would please the Lord.

Unfortunately, work is not a neutral term—it comes to us weighed down with negative associations and connotations. We've been taught by culture, and by our sinful and self-centered natures, that work is bad, an annoying distraction from our desire to enjoy the pleasures of life. It's something to be avoided and minimized, and, if necessary, endured.

But work was part of God's created order in Genesis 1 and 2, before sin's curse in Genesis 3 made it hard and onerous. When God called His completed creation "very good" (1:31), that declaration included work. God designed us originally to take pleasure in work—to create, subdue, and bring order and meaning to all that we are entrusted with by Him. God worked (2:3) to create the world, and that quality of His image is also in us as His image-bearing creatures. As mothers, created in His image, it is our privilege to model and teach a healthy attitude about work to our children.

The definition of a good work ethic does not need to be complicated. The principle is simply that work is intrinsically good, virtuous, and rewarding. We easily forget that it was only the ground that was cursed after the fall (3:17-19), not work itself. Work is still good, even if it is hard. But in a new world of no fields to plow or cows to milk or barns to build, the call to work hard because work is good is a hard sell in that new world of multiple media distractions, digital devices always in-hand, and unlimited options for leisure and pleasure.

Nonetheless, I wanted my children to see that every day, no matter how hard it was, I would make the choice to do the work of being a homemaker, wife, and mother—joyfully keeping our home clean and beautiful, making delicious meals, planning delightful outings, providing for all my children's needs, teaching them and reading to them, helping Clay do his work well, and doing my ministry well, too. I was modeling the work habits and attitudes that I wanted my children to value, internalize, and practice.

As mothers, we know instinctively that the only way our children will be able to grow, learn, and mature in life is if we do the spiritual work to "bring them up in the discipline and instruction of the Lord" (Ephesians 6:4). Our desire to see each of our children flourish and succeed in life cannot be separated from our responsibility to instruct, train, and model the biblical virtues, values, and habits in our lives that we want to see in theirs. I believe that starts with instilling a strong value for work very early.

I'm convinced that early training is foundational to instilling a value for hard work. As children learn to work with diligence and excellence, they are building a firm foundation for life. Without it, they might always struggle to find balance and sure footing in life; with it, they will have confidence to pursue any dream or goal within their reach, or even beyond it.

The first place to begin building that foundation is with Scripture, just as Jesus reminded us: "Therefore, everyone who hears these words of Mine and acts on them, may be compared to a wise man who built his house on the rock" (Matthew 7:24). Our children need to see that God has spoken wisdom about the goodness and godliness of work throughout His Word.

The need to work hard is not just an incidental idea, or something we make up to guilt our children into doing their chores. Rather, it is a part of the heart of God—He has our good in mind, even in the work we do. Having God's heart in mind by having scriptures in our minds will help us better value work.

The value of work starts "in the beginning." God blessed and commissioned His newly created creatures, Adam and Eve, to work in His new creation: "Be fruitful and multiply, and fill the earth, and subdue it; and rule over the fish of the sea and over the birds of the sky and over every living thing that moves on the earth" (Genesis 1:28). Immediately following this He declared "all that He had made" to be "very good" (1:31).

God created man and woman to work—to fill the earth, subdue it, and rule over it. Far from being a detestable duty or a punishment, God designed work to be our "very good" path to fulfillment. And again, only the ground was cursed after the fall, not work. Work became harder, but it is still good.

There are many other scriptures that affirm the value and goodness of work. Read, discuss, and memorize these passages:

- Psalm 90:17 — Let the favor of the Lord our God be upon us; and confirm for us the work of our hands; yes, confirm for us the work of our hands.

- Psalm 128:2 — "You will eat the fruit of your labor; blessings and prosperity will be yours."

- Proverbs 12:24 — "The hand of the diligent will rule, but the slack hand will be put to forced labor."

- Proverbs 14:23 — "In all labor there is profit, but mere talk leads only to poverty."

- Proverbs 16:3 — "Commit your works to the LORD and your plans will be established."

- Ephesians 6:7 — "With good will render service, as to the Lord, and not to men."

- 2 Timothy 2:6 — "The hard-working farmer ought to be the first to receive his share of the crops."

I love Psalm 128:2 because it presents the simple truth that labor is worthwhile, beautiful, and valuable. Words like work and labor can make us feel exhausted and defeated before we even begin the task. But the

Psalm points to the fruit of what labor brings. We work for a purpose. Ecclesiastes 5:12 tells us that "the sleep of the working man is pleasant." It is our job as mothers to point out the beautiful blessings and benefits that come from working hard and helping out.

I believe in rewarding children for a job well done. Our kids earned little treats or prizes for excellent work when they were young. When they were older, their diligence and faithfulness earned more freedom and our trust in their judgment as we gave them time with friends or trusted them with an independent project. At times we would pay them for special work, expecting excellence to prepare them for working for others. God meant for work to bring us fulfillment and reward. Not all tasks come with a prize, but it's a delight to affirm your children's growing work ethic by rewarding their efforts when they are young.

More than duty, or wisdom, or rewards, though, the greatest source of influence on your children's attitudes about work will be you. Before you ask your children to help out and work hard, examine your own thoughts and attitudes about work. Do you take pride in your work? Do you work with a joyful heart? Do you view your work as a blessing? Or. do you complain or gripe about the work that God has given you to do?

God has entrusted to you the stewardship of your home and children. You are called to subdue your home domain—to bring life, joy, and beauty to every part of it by doing all the work that is required to care for the place you call home and the people you call family. It is sacred work for sacred people—a holy responsibility and an offering you make to God.

God has made you the working model for your children. Little eyes are watching and little ears listening to how mama handles the tasks that each new day brings. If you complain every night about washing the dishes, your children will adopt your attitude. If you resent the work others create that you must do, your little ones will feel free to resent their duties. However, if you have an attitude of pride and joy in caring for your home, your children will follow your example. You will help shape them into independent workers with a self-perception that says, "This is my room and my house, and I want to help keep all of it clean and nice."

The cultivation of a work ethic is, in itself, a daily work. When your attitude and vision are right, all that remains is the work of faithful training—reminding your children to pick up their clothes, wash the dishes without complaint, keep their rooms clean, and complete their chores thoroughly. That kind of training wasn't necessarily my favorite part of mothering, but in hindsight it was one of the most vital.

The habits, the chores, the tasks, the projects—they all helped to train and shape my children into adults who could work hard, with good attitudes and striving for excellence, in every aspect of their lives. Their ability to work, learned in my home, has equipped them to attempt anything they can imagine. That is a gift that will keep on giving.

❤

GIVING THE GIFT OF WORK

Start with Chores

The daily work of keeping a home is a natural training ground for your children in work and diligence. Avoid doing everything for them. Instead, from the time they are small, create chores and tasks that involve them in cleaning the house, straightening rooms, decluttering closets, and preparing meals. Not only will you be training good habits, you'll also be building friendships as you work together. A few basic ideas will help provide a framework or plan as you assign different tasks to your kids.

Chore Charts: Make a basic list of responsibilities for each child. Put it on the refrigerator, or somewhere visible, so they can see what is expected of them each day. If children don't know what is required of them, then they have no goal to work toward and you have no basis on which to require their cooperation. To encourage ownership of the chore chart, get your children involved in designing one—let them choose a colorful poster board, decide on a design, and decorate it with stickers, cutouts, photos, and whatever they like so it is beautiful, colorful, fun, and exciting for them.

Incentives: There is nothing wrong with rewarding your children to help them learn to work well. Give small rewards for chores done without reminders. Create a system to earn points for each task successfully accomplished, and set different point levels for rewards from little (stickers, a piece of candy) to big (a date with mom or dad, a movie night out). Reasonable rewards and incentives parallel the blessings we enjoy from God for the obedience that He naturally expects from us. Incentives are good object lessons.

Encouragement and expectations: Have a family meeting every so often to help your children know what you expect and require of them. Encourage them when they are working well and recognize their achievement. Help them not to feel that what you require is random, but that there is a family and home system of which they are a part.

Chores for Little Children

Even at a very early age, you can begin building attitudes of helpfulness and service in your little ones. Assign age-appropriate chores to boost your children's self-confidence and help them feel that they're a necessary part of a family that works together as a team. These are also the basic daily habits of cleanliness that your children will carry with them into adulthood.

Dirty dishes: Encourage your littlest ones to bring their own plates to the sink. Older children can rinse dishes and put them into the dishwasher. To encourage family teamwork, though, your younger ones can stay involved by clearing the table, putting food in the fridge and pantry, and throwing away trash. It's all about finding ways to serve, even if they are small.

Make the beds: Making one's bed is a habit that needs to be taught early on, but once instilled can last a lifetime. From the time they are able, train your little ones to pull their sheets and covers straight, and put their pillow in place, when they get out of bed each morning.

Pick up the room: Help your children to value a clean and orderly bedroom. Encourage them to straighten their room and put away their toys each morning. Give them special baskets and boxes in their rooms to make storage easy for toys, crayons, stuffed animals, and other odd things. Make sure they hang up any loose clothing, and they make an effort to keep their closet organized. Also have them straighten the top of the desk and put loose desk items into the drawers.

Sweep to the music: Mothers cam make cleaning fun! Turn on music from Mary Poppins and give your children brooms. Encourage them to dance like Dick Van Dyke in the chimney sweepers song. An ordinary day of chores can be transformed into a musical extravaganza! Put on whatever sing-alongable music will make the housecleaning fun.

Suck it up: Even a young child can handle a handheld vacuum. Next time there are crumbs, dirt, or cereal on the floor, invite your child to handle the clean-up. They'll be helping with a necessary task, but even more they'll be having fun commandeering the handheld vacuum.

Spill ways: Raise your children with the expectation that they will clean up their own spills and messes, not just as a work saver for you, but also as training in personal responsibility for them. Fight the urge to immediately clean up spills. Have patience and help your little ones clean up their own messes.

Sock it to them: Sock matching is a groaner chore for you, but can be a fun and challenging matching game for young children. Lay out all your clean socks on the carpet or bed and ask your little one to help you match them. It can also be educational if you have them count the socks, and have them recognize patterns, textures, shapes, and colors.

Chores for Older Children

When you've put in the time and training to raise little ones with helpful hearts, they will become a great blessing to you when they are older. As my kids got older, I began to trust them with more responsibility, allowing them to own or oversee certain tasks. They also became involved in the deeper cleaning of our home and knew that they each had a certain job to fulfill.

Once-a-week deep clean: I always scheduled one morning each week to clean the house at a deeper level. As soon as they were old enough, I showed my children how to clean bathrooms, vacuum, wash windows, and do other tasks. It was training for the "Clean Team." Sarah liked wiping all the glass surfaces. Joel preferred the vacuum, and he was also my occasional expert polisher of silver. The older they got, the more discipline and initiative I expected of my children in their work. I wanted them to do it because they valued excellence and accomplishment, not just because I told them to.

Daily straightening: Twice a day—after breakfast and before dinner—I had my kids help to pick up and straighten the main rooms. For a season, Josh Groban was our sing-along soundtrack for cleaning, picking up toys, washing dishes, straightening pillows, and making everything lovely. Daily straightening was an expectation in our family and something I had the older kids take full responsibility for once they were able (to their choice of music).

Yard work: Doing yard work is a great way for older children to help out while getting some fresh air and sunshine. In the fall, raking leaves stretched them to a capacity of hard work and exercise. Shoveling snow, mowing the grass, trash, and helping with a garden are all good chores and skills to learn.

Table setting: When your children are older, you can give them free reign in setting the dinner table in a way that is beautiful and pleasing to them. This is a wonderful task for those who are creative, as they can use their eye for design in choosing dishes and silverware, candles, or a centerpiece. Allow them to decorate the table however they see fit, creating a seasonal arrangement or lighting lots of candles.

Taking on special projects: Older children are ready to take on special projects around the house. This can include anything from big projects requiring special skills, to small projects requiring time and effort. Special projects for older boys might include installing a split-rail or privacy fence in the backyard, painting a shed or garage, or framing a room in the basement. Older girls could be involved in any of those projects, or on projects inside the home such as organizing the kitchen cabinets and pantry, cataloging the library books, and others. Other less specialized projects could include cleaning and organizing the garage, purging closets of old and unworn clothing, and cataloging items to be donated for tax records.

Committing to a specific skill: Work isn't just about cleaning. As your children grow older, one of the arenas in which they must learn to work hard is toward their vocation. Help your children choose a specific skill and then be faithful to work at it long term. Whether it is taking lessons to learn a musical instrument, or practicing to excel at a sport, it all requires hard work, dedication, and commitment, skills that are crucial to living as an adult. When your children reach their goals, they will discover a healthy pride in their work that will equip them for further goals. Every child is uniquely gifted, so talk to your children about what they love. Help them to master a skill that delights them. It's not housework, but it's training and work.

Learn How to Motivate

Try this A.B.C.D.E. acrostic if you need inspiration to keep your children going.

- **A: Affirm good acts.** Acknowledge good effort whenever your child attempts any new task. Express appreciation when your child acts independently, such as picking up a food wrapper off the kitchen floor.

- **B: Boost their spirit.** Be your kids' home-style cheerleader. If they learn a new skill or task, give them an "Attaboy!" or "Attagirl!" No matter how small the task or insignificant the chore may be, always tell them, "Great job!"

- **C: Cultivate their confidence.** Tell your children how they are doing well, and be specific. Work done well that is not just seen, but recognized as good work, builds confidence and capability for taking on more.

- **D: Dedicate to training.** The best training doesn't happen passively or by chance. Set aside specific quality time for training in work so that you will have the margin and patience you need as they learn new tasks.

- **E: Encourage each child.** Learning new tasks can sometimes be frustrating and defeating for any child. Regardless of the quality of the work, encourage the effort, attitude, and the work that they are able to do.

❤

Wrapping Up the Gift

I will give my child a heart for Work by:

_____

_____

_____

_____

_____

_____

_____

_____

_____

_____

_____

_____

_____

_____

_____

How blessed are those who
observe His testimonies,
who seek Him with all their **heart**.

— PSALM 119:2 —

A HEART FOR INITIATIVE

The Gift of Taking Responsibility

Therefore, to one who knows the right thing to do and does not do it, to him it is sin.

JAMES 4:17

Freedom makes a huge requirement of every human being. With freedom comes responsibility. For the person who is unwilling to grow up, the person who does not want to carry his own weight, this is a frightening prospect.

ELEANOR ROOSEVELT

Storm clouds were forming in the autumn Texas sky as I stood at the back of the Aerostar and stared blankly at the big, black trailer hitch. Clay was out of town at a meeting, and I was preparing to drive to a speaking engagement—my first time driving with the trailer, which was a necessary evil for anyone who exhibited at events to sell books. And the trailer was not yet on the hitch. Eleven-year-old Joel saw me and ambled over to where I was standing under the carport.

"What's wrong, Mom?"

I told him I was concerned about us being able to get the trailer on the hitch.

"Daddy showed me how to hitch the trailer before he left. I haven't done it yet, but I think if I read his instructions and call him, I'll be able to get it all hooked up just right. Don't you worry. We'll get this done."

And so he did. Joel called his dad to get advice, and we were able to hook it up perfectly. He then helped me load all the books, arranging them neatly so they wouldn't shift during the drive. His diligence continued throughout the trip that followed, as did his confidence. That conference was easier because he always helped me when I had to back up or park the car, and he pitched in wherever he could. I couldn't have done it without him, and couldn't have been more proud of my Joel.

But I also felt a deep sense of joy in watching my son because I knew that he was reflecting the ideals we had trained into him. From the time he was just a little boy we had worked to instill a sense of self-government and responsibility in Joel's heart and mind. "You are a strong boy, Joel. ... You will be able to do many things if you just put your mind and will into it. ... It is a glory for a man to become self-reliant and dependable. ... We know that you will be the kind of young man that people will be able to depend upon."

We spoke those words to him regularly and persistently. We included him in our work, and encouraged him to be responsible all on his own. Every day, we encouraged him to become a master of his own heart, a man who lived by initiative instead of passivity. We wanted him to have the gift of becoming a self-governed man, not waiting to be told what to do, but taking initiative to grow and to give in every sphere of his life.

God has given us the great responsibility to subdue every aspect of the life he has entrusted to us. But far too often we sit on the sidelines of our own lives, settling into being a spectator of life around us. We watch the world from a safe distance, observing the brokenness, possibilities, and needs, while simply waiting for someone else to stand up and do God's work. In our spirits, we don't want to be disengaged, but it's all too easy to fall into that place.

It's as though we've been invited to a big dance. We're watching everyone else join in, jumping into the exciting crowd of other dancers, but we're at the edge, in the shadows, uncertain what to do. Unintentionally, we act like the proverbial "wallflower" in the dance of our own world. However, we know that's not where we want to be, so we begin to look for a way to join the dance. And that's what we need to do for our children. We're teaching them not just how to dance, but to take responsibility and initiative to join the dance. We're training them hear the music of the Spirit, step out of the shadows, and be a part of God's dance of life.

♥

When I was just out of college and a new staff member with Campus Crusade for Christ, one of my directors gave a powerful talk on the need for missionaries in then-Communist Poland. As he spoke, I felt conviction grow in my heart, and heard a voice in my head saying, "Those people need us to help them!" When the talk was over and a general invitation was given to join the new team being formed to take the gospel to Poland, I rushed forward, sure I would be one of hundreds who wanted to apply. Instead, I found that I was one of only four.

Because of the great change God's love made in my own life, I was ready to do anything to bring that love to other people. God's love made me an initiator. But many people never listen to God's call in their hearts.

As I began to raise my children, I remembered the call to ministry in Poland and the few who responded. I resolved that my children would become responders and initiators. I wanted them to be the ones who would hear the call and step forward to help. I wanted them to be active members of God's kingdom. I knew that would mean training them to take initiative in every area of their lives. As Winston Churchill said, "The price of greatness is responsibility."

Two areas of training were at the forefront of my desire to help my children become "great" in God's eyes. First, I encouraged them to discover God's unique story for their lives. It is empowering when a child realizes that God has a unique and special purpose for their life. When they come to understand they aren't just faceless workers to God, but rather are known and loved, they gain a sense of identity in Him. When they find their reason for being and purpose in Christ, they are on the way to greatness. I talked often to my children about the story God was writing with their lives.

The second area of training is that I encouraged them to discover what drives God had put in their hearts for His kingdom. I helped them identify and pursue their unique loves and passions—writing for Sarah, music for Joel, acting for Nathan, and speech for Joy. I called them to become initiators, and stewards of their unique story, message, and gifts. I explained the significance of their responsibility, and looked for ways they could serve or give. They were in training to take their places as great heroes in God's kingdom story.

Clay and I often talked with our children about the Scripture. We would read verses such as the following, ask questions, and talk about them:

- Ephesians 210 — "For we are His workmanship, created in Christ Jesus for good works, which God prepared beforehand so that we would walk in them." What good works do you think God has already prepared you to walk in? What special message or skills or gifts has God given you to use for His purposes? How can you use what He has given to you for His kingdom?

- Colossians 1:10 — "[So] that you will walk in a manner worthy of the Lord, to please Him in all respects, bearing fruit in every good work and increasing in the knowledge of God." What do you think it means to "walk in a manner worthy of the Lord"? What "good work" can you do for the Lord? How can you continue to grow in "the knowledge of God"?

- 2 Timothy 2:21 — "Therefore, if anyone cleanses himself from these things, he will be a vessel for honor, sanctified, useful to the Master, prepared for every good work." What does it mean to be sanctified, made holy? How are you "useful to the Master" right now? How are you seeking to be "prepared" to do any good work God asks of you?

One very short scripture always played a role in our training. Galatians 6:5 has the quality of a Proverb—a powerful truth in a small package. Listen to the words of this verse in several translations:

- "For each one will bear his own load." (NASB)

- "For each one should carry their own load." (NIV)

- "For we are each responsible for our own conduct." (NLT)

- "Assume your own responsibility." (GW)

God does not want us to shirk the load we have been given to carry, the responsibility we have to assume. There have been times in my life when I gave into passivity, whether in little things or big. I gave into waiting, hoping that a friend would call to ask me over for dinner. Or, I expected that someone else would start a fellowship group for my kids. Or, I saw a need in my community but waited for others to meet it. I was expecting someone else to assume a responsibility that was mine. Galatians 6:5 called me back to my need to accept responsibility and not complain. Listen to the full context of that short but convicting verse:

"Bear one another's burdens, and thereby fulfill the law of Christ. For if anyone thinks he is something when he is nothing, he deceives himself. But each one must examine his own work, and then he will have reason for boasting in regard to himself alone, and not in regard to another. For each one will bear his own load." (Galatians 6:2-5)

One of the hardest and best things I have learned is how to look into a void that could be discouraging, and create life around it instead. I had to "examine [my] own work" and learn how to bear my own load, and help bear other's burdens as I did. If I was lonely, it was my responsibility to reach out. If I wanted a group, it was my responsibility to start one. If I saw a need, I took responsibility to find a way to meet it. And I did this while my children were watching and listening. I wanted them to have a model of being "responsible for our own conduct."

It's natural for us, and our children, to occasionally throw a pity party. But moping and complaining won't change anything. One of the best gifts you can give your children is to be an initiator. Teach your children to initiate in relationships and cultivate new friendships. Teach them to start a group where there is none. Teach them to encourage the lonely if no one else will, to feed the hungry, or start an outreach. If they want friends, tell them to ask someone over. If they want a job, encourage them to hone their skills, fill out an application, and dress well for the interview.

If your children can develop the skill of initiation, they will be more likely to flourish, and to become leaders of others. Raising children who are initiators means continually challenging them to optimism, hard work, and perseverance. It was always my goal to lovingly teach and train my children, and to inspire the confidence they needed to govern their own lives and become independent and self-driven people. I wanted to influence and free my children to think, dream, and set goals all on their own.

Abraham Lincoln said: "You cannot build character and courage by taking away a man's initiative and independence." Courage and character begin with the energy of initiative. It all begins with the decisions your children make to take responsibility for their lives to live with purpose, compassion, and independence.

❤

GIVING THE GIFT OF INITIATIVE

Cultivate Ownership

Each of the following areas describes an arena in which you can help your children develop a sense of ownership for their own lives. They need to feel that they are responsible for their words, actions, and choices.

Help them dream: Make a dream board with your children to express and visualize what they are passionate about, and to create projects and set some goals to explore those passions. Use whatever works best and will be used—colorful poster board, cork board for various photos and magazine clippings, chalkboard, whiteboard. Help your children define and set some limited goals, and to make their own plans for how they will achieve those goals. For instance, if your child is expressing a desire to write, their goal could be to write a book or story, depending on their age and motivation. Other similar goals could be to learn a musical instrument, raise support for a mission trip, or start a small business. A good goal will kindle delight in your child and motivate ownership of their story. Giving your children the opportunity, freedom, and even the responsibility, to dream will plant seeds of initiation, goal setting, responsibility, and even entrepreneurialism.

Make them think: Your children will need to use initiative and responsibility in many areas of their lives—schoolwork, chores, creative endeavors, jobs, and so much more. One of the ways to encourage self-government and ownership in these areas is to train your children think—to be responsible for their own opinions, convictions, ideas, and integrity. You want your children to trust your parental wisdom and counsel, and to come to you with questions about their world—homework, friendships, curiosity, and so much more. However, rather than simply becoming the "answer mom," talk with them about their questions. Listen to their thoughts and encourage them to pursue their own answers and solutions. Share your convictions and help them to form their own. Independent action begins with independent thought.

Allow them time: Highly structured lifestyles and tightly scheduled calendars leave little room for children to practice initiation, independence, and leadership. Children, and especially boys, need freedom and time for exploration to develop skills at being self-governed. Provide age-appropriate, safe situations for them to play at home, adventure in the backyard, and try new things with their friends without constant adult supervision. Express trust in their ability to make wise decisions, and to avoid acting foolishly. Let them have hours in which they have freedom and good resources to pretend, create, and explore.

Expect ownership: As a mama of four children, I remember many moments of sibling playtime when a crashing sound would be followed by a rare and pregnant silence. Upon investigating, these situations could quickly turn into "he said, she said" narratives filled with evasion and blame shifting. This was not uncommon behavior for settling fusses as a mom. A critical part of parenting is to train our children to take responsibility for their actions by being open, honest, and willing to own their lives. No matter how long it took, I would sit with my children and talk with them until the truth was confessed and actions were owned. Similarly, if a child is avoiding a responsibility or excusing poor work, press in until they can confess the faulty or sinful behavior or attitudes, exercise correction and consequences as needed, and direct them to the proper thoughts and actions they need to own.

Explore creative arts: Whether your child is rehearsing for a play, practicing a song, writing a story, drawing an illustration, or mastering ballet, the creative arts require responsibility and dedication. Regardless of natural gifting, involvement in the arts will provide an arena for your child to take initiative, learn, and grow. Every child can find a creative art to own— writing, acting, musical theatre, instruments, children's choir or orchestra, photography, dance, drawing, painting, on and on. Whatever they choose, it is an opportunity for them to soar creatively, to test their limits, and to learn discipline and dedication.

Assign special duties: Give your children specific tasks and areas of work within the home for which they are directly responsible—a particular room, an area of the yard, care of the dog, kitchen cabinets, pantry, baking of cookies. Encourage them to do not just the minimum needed, but to become the master of their area. Challenge them to take initiative, exercise their intelligence and creativity, and consider what they do as their gift to the family.

Insist on honesty: Talk to your children about why honesty is so important in the family. Self-governance begins with ownership of one's actions and words. Your children need to know that dishonesty and deceit are not just sinful, but cowardly and self-destructive. Failure to be honest about a fault or failure is as bad as the failure that's being avoided. But it's not just about confronting the failure; it's also about showing grace. If your children understand grace and forgiveness, they will be better equipped to be honest about their own mistakes and failures, and even to show grace to the failures of others. In order to fully own what they do and say, your children need to learn from you the responsibility of being truthful.

Be patient: Self-governed children aren't developed overnight. Fight the temptation to become discouraged, and don't give up on the days when your children make a mess, tell a fib, or don't wash their own dishes (even when you've told them a thousand times). Have patience and continue to work together with them on developing these vital life skills.

Train Them in Leadership

Not every child may seem at first like a natural born leader, but every child has the capacity to learn how to think, serve, initiate, and speak like a leader. With the exception of children with a more outgoing personality and gifts, it will be natural for most children to follow others, but they can also be equipped and trained to lead others. As a mom, you can instill and release in your children the vision and confidence to lead when there is a need or opportunity. Whether they are introverted or extroverted (I had two of each), you can teach and train your children what it means to take initiative to serve others as a leader.

Begin with encouragement: Words that affirm are like a shot of secret strength into the souls of your children. When you encourage them in their efforts and affirm their initiative to create, to help, or to encourage someone else, you are helping them to love choosing what is right. Tell them what a wonderful job they have done, or how proud you are of their creativity, or how much you see them growing in faithfulness. Affirm every good thing and it will continue to grow.

Let them lead: Leadership muscles are developed by self-governing action. Allow your children to make decisions when appropriate. Perhaps one of your children has wanted to select the next film for family movie night, or maybe they can throw out a couple of ideas for what to do after church on Sunday as a family. Ask them what ministry project they might propose for the family, or let them choose the décor for their own room. When we allow our children to make simple decisions, they will be better equipped to take on the more difficult choices that life will bring.

Leaders are readers: Children need both independence of thought and an inner picture of excellence if they are going to lead well. Great books provide both. Your children need exposure to the great thinkers of the world if they are going to have minds sharpened to grapple with the difficult dilemmas and decisions of their time. But they also need the vivid beauty of classic stories to fill their minds and hearts with images of heroes who inspire them to lead, to work, and to own their own stories. Reading is a Clarkson family obsession because we all believe that stories shape souls and words form convictions in the hearts of heroes.

❤

Wrapping Up the Gift

I will give my child a heart for Initiative by:

_____

_____

_____

_____

_____

_____

_____

_____

_____

_____

_____

_____

_____

_____

_____

_____

Delight yourself in the LORD;
and He will give you
the desires of your **heart.**

— PSALM 37:4 —

A HEART FOR HOSPITALITY

The Gift of Generous Welcome

Do not neglect to show hospitality to strangers, for by this some have entertained angels without knowing it.

HEBREWS 13:2

Hospitality isn't about inviting people into our perfect homes, it's about inviting them into our imperfect hearts.

EDIE WADSWORTH

J oy lit the last candle as Sarah ladled the last bit of raspberry soup into the old crystal bowls. After fifteen years of hosting a Christmas mother-daughter tea for all of our friends, each of us now specialized in a specific task. Joy bedecked the table with delicate crystal glasses and serving pieces, and hand-painted floral china inherited from a great-grandmother. Sarah made the cold raspberry soup we had learned to love on a visit to Hungary, and also baked the cream scones that we served with clotted cream and strawberry jam. I whipped up the cold chicken salad with roasted pecans, red grapes, onions, a dash of curry, and mayonnaise and yogurt dressing. Chocolate mousse cake had become the traditional dessert with Joy's whipped cream and chocolate sauce as the adornment.

Our Christmas tea was a special annual event that had grown in importance over the years. It was in reality an appreciation tea and luncheon—a "high tea" with the china, crystal, and silver mostly for our oldest and closest Colorado friends. We also gave each mother and daughter who came a specially selected Christmas ornament to mark the event with a memorial.

In addition to our old and dear friends, though, each year we also would invite two or three women or girls who didn't have family or friends in town, or who we thought might need some special encouragement at this time of year. We considered it an outreach for the Savior during the Advent season.

This particular year, we invited a precious young woman who had grown up in such a broken home that she barely knew that kindness and thoughtfulness existed, much less for her. Her rough background had hardened her heart toward people and given her a defensive posture toward the world.

The tea went as usual that year until the end. Each person was given a small gift of appreciation and the annual ornament as we told stories of how much each person had meant to us. I noticed my special guest growing increasingly quiet, but she seemed happy amidst all the other women. After the meal, most of the women and girls chattered in the kitchen, washed dishes, straightened the table, and enjoyed the last few minutes of fellowship. In the midst of the relaxed gaggle, the young woman sheepishly walked over to me and tapped me on the shoulder.

"May I speak to you, please?"

I nodded and said, "Of course," but before she could even begin speaking she began to cry. I took her into another room for privacy where we sat together as she told me her story.

"I am thirty-five years old and I have never even had a cup of tea in a real tea cup. I've read stories in magazines about friendships like you have, but until today, I didn't even think they were possible." She paused for a moment, looked down, then back up at me. "I just want you to know that you have given me the best Christmas gift I have ever had—a sense of belonging."

In all my years of ministry, I have found that very few people actually have what many of us take for granted—a home that is a sanctuary and refuge, a safe haven where we know that we are accepted and loved unconditionally. They want that kind of home, but it is an elusive dream. It is something they hunger and yearn for, but wonder if they will ever find.

As I created a home for my own children that was rich in love, beauty, belonging, and shelter, I began to realize that this tapestry of life I was weaving was more than just for my family—it was also a gift to share with others. As we invited people into the natural rhythms of our family—meals, holiday gatherings, evenings of fellowship—they were able to taste a kind of home life and sense of belonging they had rarely, or never, known. As I included our children in this ministry of our home, I quickly realized that the gift of hospitality was one of the practices I most desired to pass on to them.

❤

Home can be one of the most deeply transformative places in the world, a refuge where lives are touched, hearts are shaped, and God is known. As a mother, you have the power to create a small, lifegiving world within your home. The rooms of your home reflect your values, your tastes, but most importantly, your love.

Home should be a beautiful place filled with God's grace—where people are loved without expectation, the table is enjoyed with all its God-given delights, memories are made because people want to remember, and the sacred sense of welcome and belonging is offered to each person who enters.

God has entrusted mothers to be the makers of homes, the cultivators of beauty, and the givers of life. This has been one of my greatest delights as a mother. However, He didn't mean us to create this abundant life and then keep it all to ourselves. When you practice hospitality, you are opening the doors of your home not just to friends, family, and fellow Christians, but also to the lost, lonely, and hurting—to strangers that we may not even know. They all need the refuge of your home and the love your family will share.

Imagine Jesus placing the key to your home directly into your hands. Would you then close the door and lock it to keep others out? Or, would you unlock and open the door to let others in? He gives you your home to bless you and your family, but also that your family then may bless others. It is one way that we may be among those who are "blessed" by the King: "For I was hungry, and you gave Me something to eat; I was thirsty, and you gave Me something to drink; I was a stranger, and you invited Me in" (Matthew 25:35). Hospitality, the "love of strangers," is one way we live out the gospel in the way Jesus pictured—we invite those who need comfort, friendship, and refuge into our home.

In the New Testament, the word hospitality means, if read literally, to show love to strangers. It means to willingly entertain those who are not of your own household. It is both commended and commanded in Scripture as something that Christians are expected to practice—it's not an option for believers. We are not those whose doors are closed to the world around us, but those who welcome strangers with open doors and open arms.

The writer of Hebrews commands his readers, "Do not neglect to show hospitality to strangers, for by this some have entertained angels without knowing it" (13:2). Hospitality is a matter of obedience, not convenience. And Peter, knowing our sinful natures, admonishes us, "Be hospitable to one another without complaint" (1 Peter 4:9). Hospitality is an attitude of welcome and acceptance. Paul adds that we should be "contributing to the needs of the saints, practicing hospitality" (Romans 12:13), and includes hospitality as a qualification of elders in the church (1 Timothy 3:2, Titus 1:8). Scripture is clear that every Christian not just should, but must, consider how to practice hospitality.

The amount of people who have told me that they never get invited into a home shocks me. What has happened to the art of hospitality by Christians? God is the great host, inviting all of us into His kingdom, to share in His feast, and live in His beautiful city for eternity. We are somehow missing the picture of divine hospitality that permeates all of Scripture, that He will "prepare a table before" us and we will "dwell in the house of the Lord forever" (Psalm 23:5-6). We are called to imitate Him in all that we do, to prepare a table in our own home so others may come in and be with us. Hospitality is a powerful way of reaching hearts, because it is expressing the heart of the God who loves us.

With a simple invitation, you can open up a new world of love—to your brothers and sisters in Christ for fellowship, to nonbelievers who need to see God alive in your home, to strangers who have never known the love and safety of a family. With a feast, or just a cup of tea, you can extend the love of Christ to a lost heart through your hospitality. And you can do all of this in your home with your children, teaching them to love and serve right alongside you.

The art of hospitality is something that can be easily learned and practiced—it is what I shared in my book *The Lifegiving Home*. But God is looking for the heart of hospitality in you—the resolve to be hospitable, to welcome strangers, because that is the heart of God. Just as he welcomed us as strangers into His kingdom and family, He wants us to welcome others into our homes and lives in the same way.

Some of my most precious memories with my children come from the times that we prepared our home for others. In opening our home to be a place of life, encouragement, and shelter for other people, we also recognized the great gift we had in each other. It was a shared experience. I have watched each of my children move into their own adult spheres and immediately carry on the hospitality they learned as children. They have learned the secret of love that is the foundation of a great home: Love exists to be shared. And hospitality is God's heart for sharing love with those who need it, whoever they may be.

❤

GIVING THE GIFT OF HOSPITALITY

Gain a Vision for Hospitality

If you are new to the idea of hospitality, the first place to begin is with Scripture. If you catch the heart of God for hospitality, and develop a vision for what it means to create a home and to invite others into it, then you will be ready to practice hospitality, and to pass it on to your children. Consider again what scripture says:

Titus 1:8 – In his letter to Titus, Paul profiles the qualifications for a leader in the church: "For the overseer must be above reproach as God's steward, not self-willed, not quick-tempered, not addicted to wine, not pugnacious, not fond of sordid gain, but hospitable, loving what is good, sensible, just, devout, self-controlled, holding fast the faithful word which is in accordance with the teaching so that he will be able both to exhort in sound doctrine and refute those who contradict" (1:7-9). Notice that hospitality is the first positive quality in contrast ("but") to the negative ones. Being "hospitable" is a qualification for someone who wants to lead within the church, the same as teaching the Word of God.

1 Timothy 3:2-7 – In his letter to Timothy, Paul includes hospitality in a longer list of qualifications for leadership: "An overseer, then, must be above reproach, the husband of one wife, temperate, prudent, respectable, hospitable, able to teach, not addicted to wine or pugnacious, but gentle, peaceable, free from the love of money" (3:2-3). It appears that one of the most important qualities of a leader is not only to be hospitable, but also to have the kind of temperament that will welcome others into his home. Leaders were expected to have open doors.

Hebrews 13:2 – The writer of Hebrews suggests that we never know who we might be sheltering when we open our homes: "Do not neglect to show hospitality to strangers, for by this some have entertained angels without knowing it." His point, in part, is that we would never want to offend an angel of God, so we should be hospitable to all people.

Romans 12:13 – In his lively list of general exhortations for the church in Rome, a decidedly non-Christian culture, Paul simply includes a description of the normal Christian life that includes "practicing hospitality." It is how we live no matter where we are.

Psalm 68:6 – In this beautiful psalm, we read that "God makes a home for the lonely" (other versions translate the text as "He sets them in families"). This brief passage is a reminder of how even God practices hospitality for our benefit.

Matthew 25:31-46 – And, of course, there is the highly convicting passage in Matthew 25:31-46 where God says that the food and comfort we offer to the "least of them," the people around us in need, are offered directly to Him. This places the idea of hospitality at the heart of the gospel message, for God invites the lost into a place where they are named and known. We are to do the same through hospitality. When we practice hospitality, we embody this truth to the world.

Start with Hospitable Dinners

Perhaps the most basic form of hospitality, and certainly the easiest to accomplish, is simply to share a meal, to break bread together. Coming to a table together with others brings people into immediate fellowship, and it is a theme mentioned often in Scripture. There is something truly beautiful about inviting guests into your home and giving them a sense of belonging at your dinner table. Be the bread-breaker, be the lifegiver, and instill those beautiful qualities in your children. As part of this practice, include your children in all of the preparations. Following are some of the tasks my own children participated in.

Decorating for guests: This was the fun task everyone loved. Depending on the season, I helped my children select placemats, pretty dishes, seasonal decorations, and candles to create a lovely table for our guests. We also made sure every common room in the house had a candle or a vase of flowers. They were so proud of the beauty they designed and loved to point it out to our guests.

Setting the table: Your children are never too young to learn how to set a lovely table correctly. Show them the different utensils and their proper placements, then let them practice by putting a folded napkin, correct utensils, and drinking glasses in place. Your younger children will take pride in knowing how to do this. When they get a bit older, have them set the table for events and parties at home. This will encourage them to take pride in their part of the hospitality and, when done together, creates teamwork that is always desirable between siblings.

Adding beauty: Inspire creativity at the dinner table by encouraging your children to help out by placing and lighting candles on the table and around the dining room, creating homemade centerpieces and other table decor, or including flowers from the family garden to create a lovely floral arrangement. Let an artistic child make place cards with guests' names for the table, or have them draw and decorate a menu to show to guests. Unless a décor decision is dangerous (flammables too near a candle flame) or will interfere with serving the meal, don't change their choices.

Plan the feast: The fun part of hospitality is selecting the tasty and colorful delicacies and delectables to put on the table. Food is a great connector of people. Involve your children in the whole meal to table process—taking orders and serving drinks, preparation and presentation, seating and serving. Allow an older child to make and bake cookies for a sweet end to the evening. Make the meal an event through which to taste and savor the gifts of food God has given to us.

Be patient: Don't become discouraged if your children aren't always perfectly perky and excited to help with the hospitality dinner tasks. It takes time and dedication to form family habits. Try putting on your child's favorite music while they set the table and light the candles to add unique personality to the moment and to keep them inspired. Remember: Hospitality is joyous! It should be a fun, rewarding experience for the family to take part in as a team.

Create Hospitable Habits

Our home always seemed to be a revolving door for guests. Whether it was a family holiday, a tea party, or a Bible study, my children knew that our home was inviting, welcoming, and ready to be filled. Hospitality was just a way of life in our home. Teaching your children simple, basic social skills will give them the confidence to be wonderful hosts alongside their parents.

Talk first: Before you throw your next big soiree, chat with your children about some of the social skills, manners, and etiquette that you've learned and practiced in your home. Discuss possible situations your children may encounter, and allow them to visualize and describe the circumstances and how they would act or respond. Be sensitive to your younger, more introverted children to explore what they are feeling. If there will be a lot of guests, let your children know so they can prepare and know what to expect.

Practice to prepare: In our family before guests arrived (or before we became guests at someone else's house) we always played "thumbs up, thumbs down."

This is how it went:

- "Do we frown and leave guests at the door?" Thumbs down!"
- "Do we smile and take their coats and show them where to go?" Thumbs up!"
- "Do we rush ahead and take the first plate of food?" Thumbs down!"
- "Do we honor our guest and let them go first?" Thumbs up!"

It's not that this practice game should be considered as any kind of strategic spiritual training, but it was a fun way to review what to do. It always helped to set our children's attitudes and expectations for whoever was coming over, or for wherever we were going. It acted like a re-set button to prepare them

Make home welcoming: We always try to write the names of our guests on a little chalkboard sign on a porch wall just outside our front door. It's a way for us to make our guests feel welcomed before they even step foot in our home. Encourage your children to create a welcoming atmosphere inside the home, too—add slices of lemon to the water, make their own inside welcome sign, make sure everyone has a name tag (for larger events), design labels for pitchers with your various beverages.

Welcoming guests: Have your children welcome guests as they come in—greeting them confidently, asking how they are, taking their coat (if it's winter), and offering them something to drink or eat. Consider each child's unique personality and strengths when suggesting and assigning welcoming tasks. Extroverted and introverted children are very different, but both types can be good hosts to make their guests feel welcome. Give them "Welcome Words" that they can easily remember and do using a simple acrostic of action verbs such as GATO: Greet, Ask, Take, Offer.

Overnight guests: If visiting friends or guests will be spending the night in our home, we want their bedroom to feel comfortable and welcoming, as though they're staying in a nice hotel (in this case, The Chez Clarkson). Along with the standard preparations such as folded towels and a bed turn down, we always put a basket in their room filled with special items—bottles of water, fresh flowers, a book or two, some roasted almonds, whole grain crackers or biscuits, and a selection of our very favorite chocolates (and a card with our contact info and WiFi login). Your children will enjoy creating welcome baskets for overnight guests. Be creative.

Thank the hosts: Whatever their assignment, always remember to encourage your children that they are doing a great job! Affirm their effort and creativity. If your children feel unappreciated, unnecessary, or overworked, they won't find joy in hospitality. You are the key to making sure your children find value and delight as they learn to serve others by being hospitable hosts.

Be a hospitable kid: Hospitality isn't just for adults. Help your children think about ways they can be a hospitable host even when it's just their friends coming over to play. It doesn't have to be complicated or awkward. It's simply thinking about their friend and what would make them feel welcome and special—greeting them at the door, offering a drink or food, suggesting things to do and letting the friend choose. Even friends want to feel welcome and set at ease.

The Key Elements of Being a Great Host

You may never know the impact of your hospitality on others' lives. When your children see the way your family values hospitality, not only will their lives be changed, they also will be changing the lives of others through the instruction you have given them. It's a ripple effect. Below, I have outlined an acrostic for "HOST" we found useful as we cultivated hospitality in our children.

H is for Home: Home is not only where the heart is, home is where family dwells, where we allow God into every little nook and cranny of our lives. It is also a gift we can give to others. Invite others into your home fearlessly, and allow your children to take part in the cultivating of true fellowship.

O is for Open: The grace of family and the gift of home is not a "right" we can take for granted, or a possession to enjoy in isolation. God has entrusted each family to create a home that is a beautiful shelter open to the world through hospitality. Part of our job is to teach our children how to open their home—open their hearts to God, open their minds to Scripture, and open their arms so others can come and find God's love, welcome, and shelter.

S is for Shelter: Not many people have a place of refuge, a beautiful oasis, or a safe haven. As a mother, you have the ability to turn your home into a sacred place of shelter where guests can become refueled, refreshed, and better equipped to take on the tasks that life may bring. Talk to your children about how important it is to make home a special, safe atmosphere in which God's love may be richly encountered.

T is for Trust: It is a blessing that we are not expected to reinvent the wheel. God isn't asking you to do crazy, unrealistic tasks in your home. The art of hospitality is within your reach, and it is within the reach of your children. Consistently read Scripture and study what God says about the home, and what He says about hospitality. Then, all you have to do is open up your heart and trust Him to love through you as you open the doors of your home.

❤

Wrapping Up the Gift

I will give my child a heart for Hospitality by:

_____

_____

_____

_____

_____

_____

_____

_____

_____

_____

_____

_____

_____

_____

_____

_____

Be strong and let your **heart** take courage,
all you who hope in the LORD.

— PROVERBS 31:24 —

CHAPTER 9

A HEART FOR PATIENCE

The Gift of Faithful Endurance

I can do all things through Him [Christ] who strengthens me.

PHILIPPIANS 4:13

Nothing in the world is worth having or worth doing unless it means effort, pain, difficulty ... I have never in my life envied a human being who led an easy life. I have envied a great many people who led difficult lives and led them well.

TEDDY ROOSEVELT

"**M**om, I just don't know if I can make it." No mother wants to hear those words over the phone from a child living several thousand miles away. I shifted in my chair and held the receiver closer to my ear as Joel told me more.

"There's just so much to be done! I have to study and prepare for finals, I have to compose several new pieces of music by next week, I'm working as many extra hours as I can, and I also have a lot going on in the house where I'm living and, Mom, I'm just exhausted. I'm getting sick and I'm worried about everything and well … what should I do?"

I took a deep breath. I prayed a silent prayer. I knew that Joel was carrying more on his shoulders at that moment than he thought he could bear. Driven to finish his degree early, he was taking a full class load, teaching music once a week at a local school, working in the college admissions office, and trying to compose the crucial piece for his senior recital.

With all that was on his plate, I knew that he must be very anxious—afraid of failure, or of not living up to own high expectations of himself. I knew his heart was probably racing, his head aching with worry. But I also knew my son. I knew his capacity. I knew he had a choice and I believed in his strength of soul to make it.

"Joel," I said, "I'm so sorry. I can't even imagine how much you must have to do and I don't know how you are able to compose such beautiful music so quickly. You have been so faithful in the past few months and I am so, so proud of you."

I heard the quiet on the other end of the phone as his breath grew slower.

"But Joel," I said, "I really believe God put you there so that you can learn everything you need to know about music. I think he's filling your heart with beautiful things and making you strong as you shoulder all this work. I know how hard everything is right now, but I believe in you with all my heart. I think you can make it. Remember your Joshua verse?"

When Joel was thirteen and struggling with a lack of confidence, he had memorized God's words to Joshua: "Have I not commanded you? Be strong and courageous! Do not tremble or be dismayed, for the LORD your God is with you wherever you go" (Joshua 1:9).

I repeated those words to him over the phone, then added, "I think God is preparing you to be a hero, to bring beautiful music into this world, but nothing good or holy is ever easy. I believe you are strong in your heart, Joel. I think you can make it."

Joel waited a moment, then responded simply and confidently, "Okay, Mom." I could hear the acceptance in his voice, and the deep, mental breath he took as he quieted his heart and accepted the challenge. We talked for a long time after that, working through different problems and concerns. I told him to rest in order to refresh his tired body. By the time we ended the call, his voice was calm, and I knew he would be okay.

Four months later, I attended Joel's senior recital concert and watched as a classical pianist performed Joel's original composition. It was quite complex and complicated, and worthy of this young man who would be honored as a "Composer of the Year" at his college. Crowds of people flocked around him afterwards, congratulating him on his work, affirming his excellence in study, friendship, and life. Joel—my tall, strong, gentle son—beamed, and I knew that he was standing on the victorious side of a great battle of soul. And he had won.

Joel had become an overcomer. This strength came after long years of Clay's and my training, after a lifetime of small choices and his own soul-deep decision to press on. Joel's choice to overcome that year was one more step toward the work and life he is living now.

It is one of my greatest honors as a mama to look at my Joel and know that he is a man God can use to accomplish great things in the kingdom because he chose to respond, to strengthen the muscles of his heart, and to patiently endure under the weight of that final month.

♥

One of the vital lessons I have tried to teach all my children is how to "fight the good fight." I knew that no matter how much love and goodness I would give to them, they would still have to learn how to live out their own story in a fallen and sometime frustrating world. If they were going to flourish and succeed, I needed to teach them to faithfully endure in the midst of hard work and delayed success—to learn how to wait, how to hope, and how to endure with grace.

We live in broken world and a hurry-up culture, both of which mitigate against the building of soul strength into the heart of your child. As a parent, it is easy to focus so intensely on giving your child what is good in life that you forget to prepare them to meet sin, disappointment, suffering, and delay. When children who have never encountered struggle confront the brokenness of life and the sinfulness of people, they are often vulnerable to a crisis of faith.

But they are also in danger of impatience, of abandoning the hard work of becoming godly or working toward a great dream because they have believed the get-it-now messages of our culture. We are a fast-food, freeway, and fun-seeking society. The cultural messages your children hear every day in media, in stores, in movies and music, is that the most important thing they can pursue is their own happiness. We live in a society that believes self-fulfillment is the ultimate goal, and then offers us a dozen things to buy or a quick fix to get us what we want.

Instead, in contrast, the road to godliness is a long one, and your children need to know that. Your children need to know that God works through seasons. That learning to wait is a large part of holiness, or creativity, or success of any kind. Teaching your child how to endure and how to wait with grace could change the whole story of their lives. This is a fallen world, and your children are guaranteed to meet pain, loneliness, and discouragement as they make their way within it, doubly so if they are pursuing holiness.

Every great athlete endures hours of hard work and discipline of the spirit to win the prize, to receive the crown. In the same way, you can train the hearts and spirits of your children to endure in the face of hardship so they can be like Paul, who "finished the course" to receive "the crown of righteousness" from "the Lord, the righteous Judge" (2 Timothy 4:7-8). You can teach them to run their race in faith, to fight their battles well, and to become heroes in the story of God.

I've known many years of loneliness, hard work, and determination. I've talked for countless hours with my children about what it means to endure, to live by faith, to walk with God in the midst of difficulty. As I've companioned my children through their own hard times, there were certain mindsets I learned through that process that helped me influence and instruct them to become those who would faithfully endure.

The first mindset was sympathy. Our hearts are made for love, friendship, and joy. In order to endure, my children needed to know that both God and I sympathized with them—we understood their struggles and frustrations. They could grit their teeth and push through times of loneliness or despair, but it would be an empty achievement without the support and encouragement of others in their lives. The foundation of their strength and determination needed to be their trust in God—in His compassion, faithfulness, and assurance to work all things together for their good—but they also needed the sympathy and support of others around them to keep pressing on in faith.

Sarah has told me how much one thing I said meant to her. During a time of intense loneliness when she doubted God's love for her, I told her that I would have faith for her while she struggled, and that my love and compassion were a picture of God's. I held her as she cried, and my words and sympathy gave her the courage she needed to keep on walking in faith. Heroes need advocates behind them, and that is one of the greatest roles that you can play as a mom.

The second mindset was to affirm my belief in my children's potential to be heroic—to articulate for them the reality that they could choose to be overcomers. In the midst of suffering, a person can take on one of two identities: the victim or the hero. Victims allow themselves to be identified and limited by their suffering; a hero endures and overcomes it.

My children needed me to articulate my belief that they could be strong—that they could choose hope, strengthen their heart muscles, and take their place in the battle for beauty, truth, and goodness. They needed me to help narrate a great story for them. As we walked together through hard times, I watched them begin to live the identity of those who could work hard, endure, and overcome hardship.

Part of this, then, was training. My children needed to own their choices of godliness. I could sympathize and affirm, but eventually my children needed to make a choice to be strong all on their own. Strength of soul requires constant practice just like strength of muscle requires regular exercise. If my children practiced self-pity, whining, and a woe-is-me attitude, I knew that they would become weak.

So I confronted my children when their sadness moved from sorrow to whining. I worked to help them change attitudes of self-pity to a focus on God's goodness. I pointed them to Scripture. I challenged them to choose, like David or Joseph, like Esther or Mary, to be heroic, because in the end, their story was in their own hands and they would answer to God for their choices.

The final mindset for teaching my children faithful endurance was to help them learn how to bring light into the darkness. In my own times of difficulty, I've learned that one of the best ways to fight despair is to create life. We love a God who looked at what was formless and void, and spoke light into the darkness, filling it with His life. We are made in His image, and we are called to be sub-creators. We are here to bring the hope of God's light and life to others.

When Sarah was deeply lonely, I began a weekly tea date with her in which we had a lovely, sit-down tea all by ourselves. We became best friends. When we moved to a new place and had difficulty finding friends, the kids and I hopped in the car and went for adventure days downtown and began to invite new friends to dinner. When Joel was unsure of his ability in music, I told him to listen to great composers and to practice every day, and he wrote the piece that gained him entrance to the school of his dreams.

❤

James, the brother of Jesus, encouraged the believers in Jerusalem with a fitting analogy: "Therefore be patient, brethren, until the coming of the Lord. The farmer waits for the precious produce of the soil, being patient about it, until it gets the early and late rains. You too be patient; strengthen your hearts, for the coming of the Lord is near (James 5:7-8)." We faithfully endure—we are patient when waiting for lifegiving rain to fall in our lives—because we can trust that Jesus is alive and coming again. Like the faithful and patient farmer, we know that a seed doesn't grow as soon as it is planted; it takes time and water.

The writer of Hebrews pictures our patient endurance as a race: "[A]nd let us run with <u>endurance</u> the race that is set before us, fixing our eyes on Jesus, the author and perfecter of faith, who for the joy set before Him <u>endured</u> the cross ..." (Hebrews 12:1-2). Jesus is our model for enduring, for being patient in our race with Him. The word for endurance means literally to "bear up under," as though we are carrying a weight. Our race can be hard, but it will be a "joy" when we have endured and finished the course. The way we faithfully endure is by "fixing our eyes on Jesus."

If your children learn to "bear up under" tasks while in your home, they will learn to faithfully endure through greater tasks and challenges as an adult. Endurance and patience will be a gift to them, something that will bring them joy. But it will also be a strength to carry them through life when they are called on by God to endure, to wait, and to work. And when they look to Jesus to endure, they will have the secret inner strength common to all heroes of faith.

❤

GIVING THE GIFT OF PATIENCE

Forming a Heart for Endurance

We want to patiently endure, but sometimes we don't. Negative attitudes of the heart—whining, complaining, discouragement, defeatism—can affect our ability to endure. As I told my children, those are all natural responses to difficulty. A supernatural response to our troubles says, "I can do all things through Him [Christ] who strengthens me" (Philippians 4:13). Endurance requires the habit of faith, which you can intentionally train into your children.

Memorize Scripture: The basis for a life of endurance is faith in a holy and good God, and treasuring the word of God in your heart (Psalm 119:11). Your children need to have Scripture in their minds so that when they meet discouragement and fear, they can speak words of truth into their struggle.

- Philippians 4:13 — I can do all things through Him [Christ] who strengthens me.

- 2 Timothy 1:7 — For God has not given us a spirit of timidity, but of power and love and discipline.

- Hebrews 10:35-36, 39 — Therefore, do not throw away your confidence, which has great reward. For you have need of endurance, so that when you have done the will of God, you may receive what was promised. ... But we are not of those who shrink back to destruction, but of those who have faith to the preserving of the soul.

- Hebrews 11:6 — And without faith, it is impossible to please Him, for he who comes to God must believe that He is and that He is a rewarder of those who seek Him.

- Hebrews 12:1 — Therefore, since we have so great a cloud of witness surrounding us, let us also lay aside every encumbrance and the sin which so easily entangles us, and let us run with endurance the race that is set before us.

- 1 Corinthians 10:13 — No temptation has overtaken you but such as is common to man; and God is faithful, who will not allow you to be tempted beyond what you are able, but with the temptation will provide the way of escape also, so that you will be able to endure it.

- Psalm 18:31-32 — For who is God, but the Lord? And who is a rock, except our God, the God who girds me with strength and makes my way blameless? He makes my feet like hinds' feet, and sets me upon my high places.

Affirm their faith: Encouragement helps your children endure by faith; positive words will narrate life into their lives. Instead of lecturing your discouraged child, or verbalizing disappointment, articulate your belief in them. "I believe you can do this. I can't wait to see what God does with your life. I'm so proud of you. Keep trying. You're getting to be so strong. Don't give up." Your words of affirmation will become solid ground they can stand on to take the next step.

Narrate hero stories: One of the best and most delightful ways you can teach your children what enduring faith looks like is to read stories about heroism. Read to your children stories of biblical heroes, of missionaries, of historical people who lived their whole lives with an enduring faith in God. For Christian stories, we loved the "Hero Tales" series by Dave and Neta Jackson. We also read books about William Wilberforce, Abraham Lincoln, and many other historical figures; men and women who influenced their generations in heroic ways. We read biographies of great scientists, artists, inventors, explorers, statesmen, and teachers who endured with faith in order to change the world through their lives. Every story you read with your children feeds their imagination of what it looks like to be brave, to be gracious, to endure hardship, and to win the race.

Forming Endurance in Young Children

Give your children bigger challenges that they can achieve quickly and easily—a goal to accomplish, a task to complete, an honor to attain—in order to teach them endurance and patience. Before they even reach the point when they will confront real difficulty in life, give your children the chance to practice fortitude through projects, goals, or dreams that will push them and challenge them. Consider the following:

Give them a challenge: Children need to own their own dreams and goals to develop a sense of self-determination. As your children grow old enough to have specific interests, challenge them to a project—a science exhibit, creating some music, writing a story, an outreach to neighborhood kids. Help your children own their ideas, to work for their creation, and to see their projects through to fulfillment.

Create a goal: When our kids were just learning to read, we made reading charts for each of them to record the number of books they had read (e.g., for Sarah, a picture of a house on a poster board, with a hundred little windows). When they reached their reading goal, they earned a special prize we had agreed on. For Joel, a day at the local theme park; for Nathan, a trip to a Christian magician's conference; for Sarah and Joy, an overnight with Mom at a local hotel or B&B. The goal sometimes took months to complete, but the prize was worth the wait and effort. As they got older, the goals got bigger—saving for a new bike, working in our office to earn money for a camp, or raising money for a mission trip.

Forming Endurance in Older Children

When your children reach an age when they're beginning to come up against struggle, disappointment, or the need for faithfulness, you can influence and encourage them to greater faith and endurance. You can be like Christ, walking with them through the difficulties, and teaching them how to walk in the light and to give light to others. That's called discipleship. Here are some ways we discipled our children:

Time to talk: Just as Jesus sometimes took a few of His disciples away to be alone with them, Clay and I made sure to plan special times with one of us when our kids were beginning to mature physically and spiritually and grapple with deeper issues. Whatever form that time would take—a coffee date, a pizza night out, an overnight away, a ministry trip together, a special event, or even a backrub at night—they were times to talk and to listen, and to really hear and understand what was going on in the souls of our kids. That would often mean longer times to talk than we had planned, but it was in those extended, and sometimes late into the night, discussions that the biggest breakthroughs and deepest insights would be experienced. There is no substitute for time and talk with a growing teen.

Time to teach: As part of that time to talk, we also began to teach and disciple our older children more intensely and deliberately. We took the Proverbs seriously that as young adults, this was the time to get serious with them about their walk with God on His path of life, the time "to give … to the youth knowledge and discretion" (Proverbs 1:4). And, of course, it was a time to help them grow as followers of Jesus, and to become "strong in the grace that is in Christ Jesus" (2 Timothy 2:1). We wanted to put as much Scripture and wisdom as we could into their heads and hearts in the years of their youth on their way to becoming adults. That meant making time, taking time, and using teachable moments.

Time to celebrate: No matter how much I wanted to, I couldn't conjure up friends for my kids when they were lonely, or make their way easier when life was hard. But I could equip them to make it through any season with grace and joy. I taught my kids how to celebrate. Pity parties and navel gazing were not in the Clarkson playbook. If my kids were down and discouraged, I listened, I hugged, I talked, and then I set them to doing something positive—have a cup of tea, watch a movie, go to an art museum, listen to music, light a candle, read a book, write a note. I consistently helped my children think about how to create life and joy around themselves, even in the midst of discouraging days. And I entered into the joy with them. Some of my favorite memories are from the days we decided to cook an autumn feast and invite all the neighbors; or bake three-dozen cookies and deliver them to friends; or visit a string of Amish farms in the Tennessee hills; or discover a tiny tea room in a nearby downtown. All of those events, and countless others, happened because of discouragement that was turned into an opportunity for celebration. God spoke light into the darkness. So did we.

Time to challenge: Your older children need challenges to develop an independent identity, faithful endurance, and self-confidence. When our children were in the early and mid-teens, we began exploring their gifts and skills for vocation. Sarah wanted to be a writer, so we challenged her to write a complete book that we would put in print. Joel wanted to be a musician, so he composed and recorded the songs, designed insert artwork, and had his album duplicated and packaged for his own CD of original music. Nate wanted to be an actor or performer, so he recorded his own songs and made creative videos. Joy wanted to be a communicator, so she was involved in musical theatre, speech and debate, and early college studies. In all of these endeavors, our children were figuring out their lives and callings. There was often spiritual struggle or confusion, but the challenge focused their hearts and minds, required them to endure with faith, and ultimately resulted in an accomplishment that gave them a sense of pride and confidence.

❤

Wrapping Up the Gift

I will give my child a heart for Patience by:

_____

_____

_____

_____

_____

_____

_____

_____

_____

_____

_____

_____

_____

_____

I will give thanks to the LORD with all my heart; I will tell of all Your wonders. I will be glad and exult in You; I will sing praise to Your name, O Most High.

— PSALM 9:1-2 —

CHAPTER 10

A HEART FOR GRATITUDE

The Gift of Living Thankfully

*[I]n everything give thanks; for this is God's will for
you in Christ Jesus.*

1 THESSALONIANS 5:18

*Piglet noticed that even though he had a Very Small
Heart, it could hold a rather large amount of Gratitude.*

A.A. MILNE, WINNIE-THE-POOH

One blustery fall day, I stood in the kitchen with my thirteen-year-old Nathan. Outside, crimson oak leaves shook on limbs and wafted in the wind as the first storm of autumn blew in with dark clouds threatening rain. Inside, all was coziness and candlelight as the other kids prepared the living room for a morning of read-aloud. Nathan and I had the important task, at least in our family, of making coffee. As we waited for the water to boil, we looked out the window.

"Look at the colors, Mom," he said, as he leaned closer to the glass. "It's amazing out there."

I nodded as the kettle shrilled and Nate turned to help me select the mugs, measure ground coffee into the filters, and pour just the right amount of boiling water. As I began to tend to the mugs of steaming coffee, Nate took his aside and, with the air of a master chef, began to craft his own perfect mug of coffee—first the requisite sugar and cream, then whipped cream artfully squirted into a pointy mound, finally a dusting of cocoa powder sprinkled sparingly on top.

"Look mom," he grinned. "It's a masterpiece."

Taking a first sip to sample his work, he rolled his eyes at its delightful deliciousness, licking the whipped cream mustache from his lips. He held the mug out to me for a toast, and then suddenly spread his arms wide.

"God is absolutely the best, Mom! He made coffee, and cream, and chocolate, and," pointing to the window, "fall leaves and storms and everything! He didn't have to make us with taste buds, but he did, and life is amazing!"

I smiled. "Nate," I said, "you are absolutely right. I hope you always remember that."

❤

Children are born with a natural capacity for wonder. They arrive in the world shaped by God to touch and taste, to explore, to see. They are like sponges, soaking up the beauty of the world as they encounter it through their senses, and they are quick to marvel at the richness of the creation around them. One of the best gifts that you can give your child is to help them protect and preserve that childhood habit of wonder, of gratefully receiving the goodness of God's world as a gift. In other words, you can teach them to live by a habit of gratitude.

Paul sets a high standard of gratitude for us: "Rejoice always; pray without ceasing; in everything give thanks; for this is God's will for you in Christ Jesus" (1 Thessalonians 5:16-18). What does it mean to live a life that is shaped by continual rejoicing and thankfulness? To give thanks to God in every situation? This is one of those Bible verses we hear but do not necessarily heed because it seems impossible.

And yet Paul's words are commands—rejoice, pray, give thanks—and he declares them all as "God's will" for us. Always. Without ceasing. In everything. These are not words we can soften or ignore. They call us to a life of spiritual awareness and activity. And if they are God's will for us, then how do we give each of our children a heart that will habitually look to God with a spirit of rejoicing and thankfulness?

If you look closely, you'll find that biblical gratitude typically begins with a personal remembrance of God—seeing His presence, goodness, beauty, lovingkindness, works, or faithfulness as He expresses Himself through us and within creation. Making that kind of gratitude a way of life means two things.

First, gratitude requires us to learn to perceive "every good thing given" that comes to us as a gift "from above, coming down from the Father of lights" (James 1:17). In other words, learning that God is good and generous. Second, gratitude requires us to meet the dark and broken things that come to us with faith and thankfulness that God is with us in those times, too (James 1:12). By teaching your children to live with this kind of gratitude, you are equipping them to meet life with a thankful, joyful, courageous, and steadfast hearts.

But as with every aspect of child training, it is a rhythm of life that has to be kept every day within your home. It is often a joyous affirmation, as it was for me with Nathan in the kitchen that day. You can cultivate wonder and thankfulness in your children simply by taking them outdoors on a nature walk, seeing the treasures that God has made, and giving thanks for them. You can nourish gratitude by the words you speak, articulating thankful wonder for all of life, from the foods and flavors we enjoy to the changing of the seasons.

You can also cultivate gratitude in your children by recognizing together the blessings God on your home and family. Let your children know when God has helped you through a hard situation financially, and let them see how He provides. Help them to see gifts of friendship, or the grace of a new community, or the provision of a new opportunity as a gift from His hand. To give thanks in everything means cultivating a view of the world in which God's goodness is never absent, but is the source of every good thing and the refuge when we need it.

But cultivating gratitude can also be a battle against discontent, boredom, envy, jealousy, and other unthankful attitudes. In a fallen world, the wonder that is the gift of childhood can be easily submerged by discontent as children are exposed to the temptations of the larger world. In our stuff-saturated, instant gratification, fast-food culture, we are driven to consume, to buy what makes us happy, and to buy it now. Children are quick to pick up on this culture. When our kids were small, if we took them to Walmart to shop with us and they encountered the overabundance of the toy section, they inevitably grew whiny afterward, wanting this toy or that thing, unhappy when we refused.

Many parents today feel that if they do not provide their children with the best toys, experiences, entertainment, lessons, or things, they are failing them. But their happiness won't come from an abundance of things and activities. James heralds a very clear warning: "Do not love the world nor the things in the world. If anyone loves the world, the love of the Father is not in him. For all that is in the world, the lust of the flesh and the lust of the eyes and the boastful pride of life, is not from the Father, but is from the world" (2:15-16). He is echoing the teaching of his cousin, Jesus, in His sermon on the mount to "not store up for yourselves treasures on earth, where moth and rust destroy, and where thieves break in and steal. But store up for yourselves treasures in heaven ... for where you treasure is, there your heart will be also" (Matthew 6:19-21). As parents, we need to guard our children's hearts against the temptations that would turn them from God.

A heart that is not crowded with attitudes of misdirected desire and discontent makes room for true joy to take root and fill those spaces. When Paul describes a heart full of the "fruit of the Spirit," joy is the second quality after love (Galatians 5:22). Love is the soil in which all the other fruits of the spirit can grow, and joy is the fruit that leads the way.

Joy grows in a heart shaped by the habit of being thankful in all circumstances of life, whether good or bad. Paul admonished the Philippians, "Rejoice in the Lord always; again I will say, rejoice!" (4:4), and then he also encouraged them to "be anxious for nothing, but in everything by prayer and supplication with thanksgiving let your requests be made known to God" (4:6). Rejoice, pray, give thanks.

So we were diligent to guard our children's hearts from the "things in the world" when they were young and most vulnerable. We were careful to address any attitudes of discontent in our children as soon as we recognized them. We talked about those attitudes with them to help them see what it might do to their hearts and relationship with God.

We wanted our children to understand that things and entertainment were not rights, and that coveting what others had, and they didn't have, breaks the tenth commandment (Exodus 20:17). We wanted to help them be content with what they had, and if they received any of those other things as special gifts, we wanted them to have a heart that would simply be joyful and thankful for them. We wanted to be sure we were helping them to make room in their hearts for the Spirit of God to grow the fruits of "love, joy, peace, patience, kindness, goodness, faithfulness, gentleness, self-control" (Galatians 5:22-23).

❤

Thankfulness is not always about big things, but is just a frame of mind about everything. Sarah distinctly remembers the time at a picnic when a friend of mine handed her a whole can of root beer. In our financially lean years as a family, she was used to splitting drinks with her brothers, so she turned to me with wide eyes and asked, "Do I get to drink the whole thing by myself?" She still recalls the pleasure of that drink and told me recently of a conversation she had about it with a friend.

"Mom," she said, "we both decided that we were really thankful to have grown up in our parents' lean years, when we couldn't afford everything. It taught us to enjoy life, to really see every gift, every meal out, or trip, as something special."

A grateful heart is a humble heart, one that does not demand but receives, and gives again, with joy. A heart attitude of gratitude also taught my kids and me, as I worked to model it to them, how to face suffering when it comes, which it will to everyone. Though gratitude at first glance seems to be only about all the good things we enjoy from God, it also is intricately connected with how we deal with the hard, broken, and bad when it comes into our lives. The natural human response to suffering and difficulty is sorrow. There is nothing "unthankful" about sorrow, unless it is allowed to move into despair, and even disbelief.

As we move through the sorrow in our lives, we have the choice to respond to suffering with faith, to look beyond our grief to the God whose love promises to heal and redeem all that is broken. In my life, I have found that one of the most powerful ways of acting out this faith is through affirming God's goodness right in the midst of struggle. I choose to celebrate and be thankful for the goodness of God.

My kids told me recently how much they learned as they watched me handle one particularly hard evening in our family. There was a period of several months when Clay had to be gone five days a week and I was by myself with the kids. We were tight on money, in the midst of a church dispute, and I was struggling with health. One night, after a particularly hard day, Clay left for his workweek and I was left once more with the kids. As I shut the door, I knew that they were watching me, wondering if I would be sad for the rest of the evening.

I sighed, turned around and said, "Okay everyone, let's have a picnic on my bed and watch a movie tonight. Joel and I will get cheeseburgers. Sarah, you make cookies. Nate, you and Joy pick a movie." Their faces went from apprehension to excitement in an instant. That night, we had a small feast on my bed, cuddled, and watched an old adventure movie. They told me recently that evening helped them understand what it meant to create light in the midst of darkness; to choose joy, the evidence of a grateful heart.

To be thankful at all times is to "walk in the Light as He [God] Himself is in the Light" (1 John 1:7a). To give thanks is to dwell in the joy of God, "for the joy of the LORD is your strength" (Nehemiah 8:10). To be thankful is to be in fellowship with "the Father of lights, with whom there is no variation or shifting shadow" (James 1:17). To live in wonder and thankfulness is to encounter the beauty and grace of God every day.

A thankful heart is a source of courage for facing the battles of this life. By giving your child the gift of a grateful heart, you are equipping them to meet every aspect of their life with a secret source of strength, so they can say: "The LORD is my strength and my shield; my heart trusts in Him, and I am helped; therefore my heart exults and with my song I shall thank Him" (Psalm 28:7).

❤

GIVING THE GIFT OF GRATITUDE

Cultivating Wonder Naturally

One of the most enjoyable ways to nurture a grateful heart in your kids is simply to give them the time and space to wonder and work. You're creating a time for creativity, giving your children the freedom to explore, and making room for their curiosity. But most of all, you're expanding their hearts with a bigger and more personal view of God. Here are some ways we did that with our children:

Light Times: This is free time for reading, writing, creative exploration, music, art, or whatever interests your child. Declare a certain time each day as "Light Time" when all distractions are minimized—turn off all devices and screens, put the phone on mute or hold, get whatever is needed from the kitchen (drinks, snacks, etc.), and make sure everyone has a special place to be for the Light Time. Then turn on the "Light" and see what shines.

Drawing: Every child should draw. It is an exercise of expressing what the mind sees rather than knows. Equip your kids with notebooks and pencils (and a snack to sweeten the deal) and send them outside to collect five treasures and to draw them in their notebooks. Encourage them to look for the small details. Ask them to identify at least three things that their treasures say about the good God who created them.

Feasting: Let your children help you plan a feast of their favorite foods and beverages. Get them involved—shopping for ingredients, helping with cooking, making the food flavorful and colorful, setting the table and room. Talk with them about the variety of tastes and scents in the different foods, and what they say about God. Make the feast a celebration of God's bounty, creativity, and goodness.

Stargazing: On a warm night, take your kids out to a dark place (no city lights), put a blanket down to lie on your backs, and engage in stargazing. Use a mobile app such as Night Sky or Sky Map on your smart phone to identify constellations, planets, stars, and galaxies. Choose ahead of time some appropriate stargazing music to play, and have some stargazing snacks ready to eat. Read Psalm 19: "The heavens are telling the glory of God; and their expanse the work of His hands. Day to day pours forth speech, and night to night reveals knowledge" (19:1-2). Talk about what everyone hears God saying from the heavens and the stars.

Adventuring: Take your kids for a mountain (or ocean, or forest, or country) drive and picnic. Put on music you all enjoy and sing along out loud. Call it a day of celebration and tell your children to observe all the ways that God has created good things for us to enjoy—food, music, family, earth, sunsets, wildflowers. Take lots of photos to create a collage, album, or slideshow to remember your day.

Articulating Thanks and Joy

Words are powerful. What and how we speak creates a verbalized narrative that reveals what we think about life and God. Help your children to value words by reading out loud with them the Word of God, great literature, inspiring poetry, and thoughtful articles and essays. Help your children to articulate the wonder they see and how God is revealed through it. Practice with them the habit of expressing joy and thanksgiving when they sense it in their spirits. To paraphrase Paul, "Gratitude comes by hearing." Here are some other suggestions:

Give thanks: Make a family practice of identifying the good things that happen in your life. Whether at dinner time, bedtime prayer, or simply in the car, practice the habit of expressing thanks for friends, meals, beauty, and experiences. Create a culture of spoken gratitude in your home—if there's thankfulness on your heart, it should be on your lips.

Write thank-you notes: Teach your kids to write thank you notes. This is a basic of etiquette and training, a skill that will take them far in adulthood. But it is more than just that. It is also a powerful way of helping them to express thanks, to recognize and honor the generosity they meet in others. Remind them to say thanks not just for the gift or experience, but also for the person and how God has used them. Writing a thank-you note is also training in how to have a thankful and joyful spirit.

Thanks for bedtime: As part of bedtime prayers, have your children thank God for the blessings and beauties, small or large, that they have encountered during the day. One of my friends keeps a yearly planner by her bed, and uses the spaces for each day to list what she was thankful for that day. You could keep a similar book for your children, a record of blessing they can look back on as a history of God's goodness in their lives.

Stop complaining: When your child is whiny or discontent, ask them to name ten things that they are thankful for instead of complaining. You will probably need to be patient to break through the negative attitude, and to help them get the list going, but be positive and affirming as they begin to name things. If you're joyful, they'll move toward joy. Rejoice!

Enjoying Special Celebrations

What better day than Thanksgiving to practice the art of gratitude? Isn't it delightful that we have a national holiday set aside just for giving thanks! Even though it's not a Christian holiday, it is deeply rooted in biblical concepts and principles, so it's only right for us, as believers, to celebrate the day as giving thanks to God. However, we shouldn't rely on that day alone to celebrate our thankfulness. There are other special days and traditions you can celebrate to add more times of thanksgiving throughout the year for your family. Here are some ideas we have enjoyed as a family:

Family Day: Create an annual Family Day just for your family. In our house, we put aside a Saturday near our anniversary. We start with homemade cinnamon rolls, milk (for dunking), and coffee. As we enjoy our rolls, we start sharing and listing out (Dad's job) all the ways that God has been faithful to our family in the previous year—jobs acquired, new friends made, health issues resolved, opened doors, providential provisions, traveling mercies, and more. We list it all out and write it all down so we can be aware of the goodness and faithfulness of God every year in our lives. They are our "memorial stones" like you read about in Joshua chapter four. We have a family time of prayer and praise afterwards. It's our high day of giving thanks to God.

Birthday breakfast: Birthday mornings in the Clarkson home always follow the same structure and ritual. First, the celebrant comes to a table filled with presents and Happy Birthday is sung. Then, we have the traditional birthday breakfast feast of eggs, bacon, hash browns, and homemade cinnamon rolls. More hot tea or coffee is poured and presents are opened, appreciated, and put aside. Then, we go around the table and each person says to the birthday child what they think is special, worth praising, or why they are thankful for them. Finally, we ask what we can pray for the child for the year ahead, and then we pray for them. It is such an anchor in our family experience that our grown children still demand it when they are home for a birthday.

Weekly celebration: Set aside one dinner each week, when everyone can be at the table, as a time of joy and thanks. Whether it's a Sunday dinner or a high tea, make that time a feast that everyone will enjoy. Let each person share the highlights, joys, thanks, and wonders of their week, and share prayer requests and praises. If you feel creative, have "thank you" tokens that are placed on the table or in a jar for each prayer, or have each person light a votive or other candle for their request. End the time in family prayers of thanks and joy.

Responding to Grace Gratefully

It is easy for children to be unaware of how blessed they are, especially in our culture of excess and consumption. Periodically, gently expose your children to the harsher realities faced by children around the world. Read some stories or materials, or watch some informative videos (not the sensational kind) to help them become more aware of how other children in poverty in our country or in third world countries live. Talk with your children about how their experience compares, and what their response to God should be.

Sponsor children: If you sponsor a child overseas through Compassion or World Vision, find pictures and information on your child—where they live, what their local culture is like, and what their living conditions are. Ask your children to try to compare a day in the life of their sponsored child with a day in their own lives in America. When your children are old enough, encourage them to earn and save money in order to sponsor a child on their own.

Simple meal: Occasionally, plan a "Third World" dinner night. When I did this, I would make a very simple dinner such as rice and beans with hard bread, and we would spread blankets on the living room floor as a family to eat our dinner by candlelight. The simplicity and lack of usual abundance helped give our kids a small taste of the simpler, starker realities that children live with in other parts of the world. You can also do this to replicate a meal from the country where you have a sponsored child. The sponsoring organization can provide that information for you.

❤

Wrapping Up the Gift

I will give my child a heart for Gratitude by:

_____

_____

_____

_____

_____

_____

_____

_____

_____

_____

_____

_____

_____

Your word I have treasured in my **heart,**
that I may not sin against You.

— PROVERBS 119:11 —

CHAPTER 11

A HEART FOR READING

The Gift of a Storyformed Life

A Bonus Chapter by Sarah Clarkson

*And do not be conformed to this world, but be trans-
formed by the renewing of your mind …*

ROMANS 12:2

*How many a man has dated a new era in his life from
the reading of a book.*

HENRY DAVID THOREAU

A few years ago, I sent a copy of *Anne of Green Gables* to a little girl I had never met and probably never will. All I knew about her was that she was eleven-years-old and that she'd never heard of my favorite childhood literary heroine, Anne Shirley. I met her mother on a flight to Canada, discussing with her the merits of Prince Edward Island, the tiny island in the Maritimes where Lucy Maud Montgomery set the story that has companioned generations of young girls through their childhood and adolescence. The mother, in all her trips to that island as a flight attendant, had never heard of Anne. When she told me of her daughter, I simply couldn't bear the thought of a little girl growing up without the world offered in the Anne books. I got her address and shipped a copy off as soon as I got home.

I tell this story in *Read for the Heart*, my guide to children's literature, because that encounter was one of the kindling causes behind the writing of that book. For days after that airplane conversation, I was troubled. At first, I couldn't quite understand why. After all, I told myself, *Anne of Green Gables* is just one story. Beautiful as it is, could it really change a little girl's life?

When I returned home and began to go back through the favorite stories of my childhood, mulling the idea of writing a guide to children's books, I realized the cause behind my troubled soul. As I delved back into the story-worlds that companioned my girlhood, encountered the characters that were the heroes and heroines looming large in my imagination, I realized how deeply the books I read had shaped my vision of life. My own ideas of courage, of creativity, of friendship, of beauty, were greatly formed by the stories that filled my mind and heart in my earliest years.

The distress I felt for that nice flight attendant's daughter came from my realization that Anne's world created a world within my heart that influences the way I live today. It's a world I think every girl needs. The community pictured in the Anne books, the way Anne encounters creation as a living thing, the "kindred spirit" friendships she sees as treasures, her lively imagination—each of these influenced the way I live, relate, and envision my own life as an adult. Though her world was not my world, her story formed my story.

When I mentioned this to several writer friends currently at work on children's books of their own, they immediately agreed. The Anne books formed the sensibilities of generations of girls, affirming family, beauty, community, and imagination. But, as one friend pointed out, Anne's story has begun to fade too rapidly from the literary scene. The stories forming the hopes and expectations of girls today, whether in print or media, are trending strongly toward teenage romance, vampire adventures, the supernatural, and pure fantasy types. Anne has been pushed aside by a shifting culture.

My friend said to me, "What different worlds girls today have in their souls." Her observation is key, and it drives one of the reasons I am passionate about speaking to parents on the vital importance of giving the gift of great stories to their kids, especially in books.

We are all story-formed souls. We live within the story of our own lives, and are shaped by the stories of others, and by the stories we read. Each story that a child encounters in their earliest years—each image conjured by their imagination, each character encountered, each landscape imagined—shapes the person that child will become.

First, stories form a child's expectation of the world. What is required of a good person? What does it mean to be good? What does it mean to be heroic? What is beautiful? What actions are good, and what do those look like? What is evil? What are the consequences of certain choices?

Every good story a child reads provides the answers to these fundamental questions about the nature and goal of life. There is no such thing as a neutral story. Stories always communicate, and they speak in the powerful language of image. In a story, abstract ideas like good and evil are enfleshed in the actions of characters, reflected in the beauty of landscapes, and revealed in the choices and consequences of each person in the story. Great stories communicate a certain idea of what it means to be human and what ought to be desired, sought after, and fought for in the world. Thus, it matters immensely that children read great books because every story that they encounter helps them to answer those fundamental questions concerning who they will be and what they ought to become.

Stories are your ally as a parent in forming your children to have a moral imagination. Stories help them to envision goodness, and they also make it desirable by clothing it in familiar and faraway lands and times, and in appealing characters of humor, fire, and depth. Good stories help children to "taste and see" what it means to live life to the fullest and with integrity.

But the second thing that stories do is that they help your child to form an interior world. This has implications both spiritually and educationally. We live in a world of such frenetic activity, such constant outward expression, and such all-immersing technology that it is easy to forget the life of the mind, the inner world of the soul. Children especially are increasingly caught up in the distraction of technology, and in the cultural push toward minute-by-minute entertainment. This has consequences on several levels.

First, on an educational level, numerous studies have shown how necessary reading is to educational success. Media technology distracts the mind, while reading develops the brain. Some studies suggest that reading is the golden key in helping children to succeed, the first skill they need in order to grasp the ideas and concepts they encounter in every other subject.

But on a more spiritual level, when children live hurried, distracted, or technology-driven lives, the imagination gets entirely neglected. The human imagination is a powerful force, one that parents must cultivate in their children if they want to nurture creativity, independence of thought, and even spiritual sensitivity. The imagination is an interior realm where creativity begins, where ideas are conceived, and where children encounter the mystery of realities that exist beyond the confines of what they merely see.

Great books enter into the process of cultivating imagination because they are works of imagination. When you give your child a good story to read, you are giving them the opportunity to exercise their brain by transforming the words they are reading into pictures within their minds. Stories give children space in which to think, and much needed quiet in which to go deeply within their own thought. Educationally, this provides the brain the chance to encounter new language, to sift through new ideas, and to add new concepts to its store of knowledge. Spiritually, stories help your children create a rich interior world, an imagination stocked with the imagery and color of your child's own inner creation. Stories create space in a hurry-up world in which a child can wonder, imagine, and eventually create.

"Today a reader, tomorrow a leader," (Margaret Fuller) is a quote passed around in many forms, but one that will continue to be repeated because of its truth. The act of reading and the cultivation of imagination will equip your child with the vocabulary, the vision, and the inner world necessary for them to think and lead independently within their own world. Great stories will shape the great story you want your children to live.

My own parents grasped this early on. I count it one of the greatest gifts of my life that I was raised in a home crammed with books. The fact that my mom required me to read every single afternoon began a lifelong habit of reading in me that I cannot escape to this day. My parents were careful to choose books of literary and spiritual excellence, and they gave me free reign throughout my childhood in exploring the treasure on offer in our library.

As an adult now, I can honestly and very passionately say that the stories I read as a child shaped my spirit to a taste for courage and innovation. Stories have companioned me through times of struggle, giving me a vision to work toward. And they have shown me what is possible for me to become. There are few greater gifts you can offer your child than the gift of a reading life. I am eternally grateful to my parents for a childhood crammed with good books. Yours will be too. I guarantee it.

❤

GIVING THE GIFT OF READING

Forming a Storyformed Lifestyle

Read every day: Habits are the hardest things to begin, and the easiest to carry out once they are well founded. Help your children to form a lifelong habit of reading by encouraging them to read at least a half-hour every day. Any kinds of books with well-written and conceived morally good content will work—picture books, story books, historical fiction, classics, poetry, mystery, biography, or whatever tickles their fancy. Appealing books with topics that appeal to your children will help them begin that habit of reading each day. When they are older, up the challenge to an hour of reading daily.

Read aloud a lot: Not all children will be natural readers. And even for those who are, the gift of daily read-aloud times with a parent provides a companionship in the reading lifestyle that makes it a joyful practice. But it is also an important practice for learning. Hearing well-written words read aloud is a different process for the brain than reading words on a page. Listening, attending, and internalizing are skills just as important as reading itself. Create a culture of reading in your home by making read-aloud a daily, family rhythm.

Read by listening in: Do you spend any time in the car? Are you going on a road trip? Put away the digital devices and get everyone together in listening to an audiobook. Choose intriguing stories or humorous ones, tales that will get the whole family eager for another jaunt in the car. Some of our audiobook family favorites include classics such as *Cheaper by the Dozen, The Treasure-Seekers, The Hobbit,* and *Where the Red Fern Grows.* We also all loved the dramatized "Chronicles of Narnia" produced by Focus on the Family for their "Family Radio Theater" series. Once a good story gets going, the hours and miles will pass quickly and delightfully, and the travelers will soon be asking for another.

Enjoy your local library: Make a trip to the library a regular family event. Take your kids to the children's section and let them choose several books of their own to check out (in addition, of course, to those you choose for them!). Make it a treasure hunt, an expedition into the storied land of imagination and history. You never know what you'll find there! And get to know your librarians as literary Sherpas, always ready to help you find your way through the forests and fields of books in their world. Take your children to special events and story times that make the library a fun place to go. If you ask your children what they want to do and they say, "Let's go to the library," consider that a major mom win.

Books make the home: I've always loved the Anna Quindlen quote, "I would be most content if my children grew up to be the kind of people who think decorating consists mostly in building enough bookshelves." Indeed. One of the best ways to cultivate the reading life in your home is simply to have books all around. This doesn't mean decorating only with bookshelves, but it does mean picture books in baskets, lower shelves of children's classics, and coffee tables with a few picture books or art tomes open. Most important, don't neglect to start a home library as soon as you can. All you need to start are a couple of good bookshelves. Once you get going, you'll be looking for more bookshelf space. Make books accessible, present, and inviting.

Get in the habit of used books: The process of outfitting your home with books doesn't have to be an expensive habit. Go on bookish treasure hunts for used books at garage sales, on eBay, at library sales (great resource!), and in your local used-books stores. You can also search for bargain-priced copies of out-of-print and hard-to-find books for your family on Amazon.com and abebooks.com. There are countless inexpensive ways that you can build an excellent home library. Like rescue dogs from the shelter, consider used books to be "rescue books" that you are adopting and taking home to love and enjoy.

Enjoy reading dates: Some of my favorite memories from childhood are from the times whn my mom took me out to a café, or set up a mom-and-me only time in our home in order to read aloud favorite stories such as *Little Women, The Girl of the Limberlost,* or *The Little House on the Prairie.* The delight of savoring a story with my mom remains in my heart to this day.

❤

Wrapping Up the Gift

I will give my child a heart for Reading by:

_____

_____

_____

_____

_____

_____

_____

_____

_____

_____

_____

_____

_____

_____

But I have trusted in Your lovingkindness;
My **heart** shall rejoice in Your salvation.
I will sing to the LORD, because He has dealt
bountifully with me.

— PSALM 13:5-6 —

About the Author

Sally Clarkson is the mother of four wholehearted children—Sarah, Joel, Nathan, and Joy—all grown and walking with the Lord. She is a popular conference speaker and the author of numerous books on Christian motherhood, parenting, and the Christian life. She is an active blogger and podcaster on her personal website at SallyClarkson.com.

After graduation from college, Sally ministered to students at the University of Texas in Austin, built a ministry to women in then-Communist Eastern Europe for three years, and returned to start a ministry to single adults and executive women in Denver, Colorado. Since her marriage to Clay in 1981, she has continued to minister to women and mothers.

In 1994, Clay and Sally started Whole Heart Ministries to encourage and equip Christian parents to raise wholehearted children for Christ. Since 1996, Sally has ministered to thousands of mothers through her conference and event ministries, spoken internationally on four continents, and her books have been translated into Chinese, French, Dutch, Korean, and other languages. Sally also trains leaders for Mom Heart Ministry, which has thousands of moms involved in small groups, and has generated a Mum Heart Ministry with events and groups in Australia, New Zealand, England (UK), Scotland, and South Africa.

Sally loves the companionship of her children and husband, thoughtful books, beautiful music, holiday traditions, classic British drama, strong English Tea, candlelit dinners at home, walking, and traveling. She and Clay live in Monument, Colorado in the shadow of Pikes Peak.

❤

But the seed in the good soil, these are the ones who have heard the word in an honest and good **heart**, and hold it fast, and bear fruit with perseverance.

— LUKE 8:15 —

Recommended Resources

We so appreciate your purchase of *10 Gifts of Heart*. Please also visit Sally on SallyClarkson.com, where she blogs and podcasts regularly on motherhood, discipleship, and faith. You might also enjoy the following titles on motherhood, parenting, and the Christian life from Sally and other Clarkson family members and friends:

The Mission of Motherhood
Sally Clarkson (WaterBrook Press, 2003)
Sally explores the "big picture" biblical design of God for motherhood, a vision that transcends cultures and current trends. Drawing on challenging insights from Scripture and her own experience as a mom, Sally paints a biblical and very personal portrait of motherhood that reveals the heart of God for all mothers of all times.

The Ministry of Motherhood
Sally Clarkson (WaterBrook Press, 2004)
In a personal and devotional style, Sally addresses how a mother can spiritually shape and influence the precious lives entrusted to her care by looking to the life and ministry of Jesus as he trained his disciples.

Desperate: Hope for the Mom Who Needs to Breathe
Sally Clarkson and Sarah Mae (Thomas Nelson, 2013)
Follow the heart-to-heart conversations of Sarah Mae, a young mom in the trenches with three children, and Sally, a seasoned mentor mom of four grown children, as they discuss the eternal value of motherhood, the difficulties of being a good and godly mom, and the grace to be found in the midst of the journey.

Own Your Life
Sally Clarkson (Tyndale, 2014)

With over forty years of ministry on campuses, in the mission field, to women and mothers, and as a speaker and author, Sally challenges others to take hold of their lives by faith. She explores what it means to live with deep intention, bold faith, and generous love.

The Lifegiving Home
Sally Clarkson and Sarah Clarkson (Tyndale, 2016)

Sally's and Sarah's vision for creating a home to be a place of belonging and becoming—to fill spirits, not just of those who live within it, but all who come into its doors. Personal insights and stories about that lifegiving home from Sally, the mother who created it, and Sarah, the daughter raised in it.

The Lifegiving Home Experience
Sally Clarkson and Joel Clarkson (Tyndale, 2016)

A companion "12-Month Guided Journey" to *The Lifegiving Home* about how to create your own lifegiving home. Written by Sally, with her son Joel Clarkson.

Different
Sally Clarkson and Nathan Clarkson (Tyndale, 2017)

This is the story of an outside-the-box kid (Nathan) and the mom who loved him (Sally). Their back-and-forth discussion style in this different kind of book is an insightful and vulnerable exploration of the experience of being that "different" child, and being the mother who raises that child.

A Different Kind of Hero
Sally Clarkson and Joel Clarkson (Tyndale, 2017)

A companion study to *Different* that is a "guided journey through the Bible's misfits." Sally and Joel examine the stories of biblical characters who didn't quite fit the mold of the world around them, in order to learn what it means to be a different kind of hero.

Your Mom Walk with God
Sally Clarkson (Whole Heart Press, Third Edition, 2016)
Sally's personal stories and biblical insights from over twenty years of parenting on what it means to walk with God as a mother on the "path" you have been given. Sally shows how to walk that "path" with purpose, assurance, trust, and heart. Originally published as *The Mom Walk*.

Seasons of a Mother's Heart
Sally Clarkson (Apologia, Second Edition, 2009)
Sally's first book (1998), written with homeschool mothers in mind, filled with stories, biblical insights, and personal reflections from four seasons of motherhood. Each chapter is followed by a full Bible study and discussion questions.

Educating the WholeHearted Child
Clay Clarkson (Apologia Press, Third Edition, 2011)
Clay's exploration and explanation of the WholeHearted Learning model, a discipleship and literature-based approach to Christian home education that starts with the "Christian home" before moving to "home education.

Read for the Heart
Sarah Clarkson (Apologia Press, 2009)
Filled with over a thousand book recommendations and reviews, insightful essays, and personal stories, Sarah provides a guide for parents who want to navigate the wonderful world of children's literature. This book is a wonderful companion guide to *Educating the WholeHearted Child*.

Caught Up in a Story
Sarah Clarkson (Whole Heart Press, 2013)
Sarah's short but visionary exploration of what it means to foster a "storyformed life" of great books and imagination with your children. Using the five movements of a story, she examines the soul-forming power of story to help children imagine, and live, a great story of their own.

Our 24 Family Ways: A Family Devotional Guide
Clay Clarkson (Whole Heart Press, Third Edition, 2014)
Clay's "just add Bible" family devotional and discipleship resource based on twenty-four statements of biblical family values. Complete with daily devotionals, character quality definitions, story starters, and line-art illustrations for your children to color. *Kids Color-In Book* also available.

Heartfelt Discipline
Clay Clarkson (Whole Heart Press, Third Edition, 2014)
Clay's insights into what Scripture really says about childhood discipline, parenting on the path of life, and reaching the heart of your child. A full biblical exploration of what God says, and doesn't say, about the discipline of young children.

Taking Motherhood to Hearts
Sally and Clay Clarkson (Whole Heart Press, 2015)
Many mothers long for fellowship with other moms but don't know how to find it. That's why we started Mom Heart groups. This guide will show you how to start, lead, and tend your own Mom Heart group to find the fellowship you need.

About Whole Heart Ministries

Keeping Faith in the Family

Whole Heart Ministries is a Christian home and parenting ministry founded by Clay and Sally Clarkson in 1994 to help Christian parents raise wholehearted children for Christ. Its current ministry initiatives include: Sally Clarkson Ministry, Mom Heart Ministry, Storyformed Project, Family Faith Project, and WholeHearted Learning Project. Through Whole Heart Press we create and publish new books and resources for Christian families, and find and reprint selected public domain books. Whole Heart Ministries is a nonprofit, 501(c)(3) tax-exempt Christian ministry.

Whole Heart Ministries
PO Box 3445 | Monument, CO 80132
719-488-4466 | 888-488-4466
whm@wholeheart.org | admin@wholeheart.org

Ministry Websites:
WholeHeart.org
SallyClarkson.com
MomHeart.com
Storyformed.com
FamilyFaithProject.com

I pray that the eyes of your **heart** may be enlightened, so that you will know what is the hope of His calling, what are the riches of the glory of His inheritance in the saints, and what is the surpassing greatness of His power toward us who believe.

— EPHESIANS 1:18-19A —

Made in the USA
Lexington, KY
27 June 2017